Lighten Up

Messages From The Spirit World

Dan Farish

Lighten Up

Messages From The Spirit World

Dan Farish

Copyright © 2012 Dan Farish

ISBN 978-0-983-5811-4-7

Library Congress Control Number: 2012951449

Whidbey Island, Washington • USA

Dan Farish was born in 1955 and raised in a working class Boston suburb, along with two sisters. His first book, *3 Steps To Recovery*, won a 2012 Reviewer's Choice Award.

More stuff from Dan -

www.3stepstorecovery.com

www.breakingfreeaddictionrecovery.com

T 87

PUBLISHING
COMPANY
Freeland, Washington • USA
T87publishingcompany.com

The book is already a reality here in our world. Now it's up to you to give it flight. Yes, here it is bound in sky blue with golden writing on the cover. It is given the name of LIGHTEN UP. We like that and congratulate Danny on the choice of title. The book will be obedient to Love and log many readers.

Foreword

Although I am in frequent contact with Dan Farish, the first I heard about his second book arrived in an email he sent, asking me to write its foreword. I agreed immediately, before reading a single word of his book.

Dan is full of surprises. He was once a fully-fledged alcoholic who became a take it or leave it social drinker. He's the only good writer I know who has never been much of a book reader and he is someone who, at first glance, you'd least expect to be spiritual.

Dan has always been complimentary about the help my writing course gave him before he wrote his first book. In truth, he was given little more than a few pointers. As far as I can see, he's one of those rare people who sucks up knowledge effortlessly and doesn't need to be told anything twice. He knew what he wanted to write and just needed someone to give him a few suggestions to get him going. My hunch is that this is how he mastered cooking and managing pizza restaurants and was also the way he learned about tiling and grouting, which made him successful in that field, as well.

In his last book, 3 Steps to Recovery, Dan described how he overcame a twenty-year addiction to drink and drugs, literally overnight, following a profound spiritual experience. That was almost two decades ago and those toxic substances have never recovered their hold on him. It's an utterly compelling story and worth reading for the autobiographical content alone. I continue to nag Dan to re-brand the book as a memoir and get it out of the self-help ghetto in order to find the millions of mainstream readers it justly deserves.

Dan's spiritual experiences didn't end with his first one, however. Other inexplicable events have been happening to him ever since. For instance, as you will discover when you read Dan's introduction, he was told he would meet a person called Peter, who would help him write his book in a place called St Heliers, which is a district in Auckland, New Zealand. At that time I was living in England and Dan resided in the States. By the time we had our first face-to-face encounter, we had established contact by email and phone and Dan was well into writing his book. It came at one of the lowest points in my life. My then wife was a week or two from moving out our home, we were desperately trying to sell our house before the bank repossessed it, and I'd badly fallen out with members of my family back in the UK. I was in a strange country, didn't know anyone, and all my close friends were about as far away as one could be. Over the next few months Dan became my guardian angel. He phoned me a couple of times a weeks to see how I was, arrived on Saturday mornings with a collection of morale boosting pastries, and generally helped me in all sorts of practical, financial and emotional ways that made the difference between having a hard time and having a ball.

I'm always happy to read anything Dan writes. Apart from being very well written, it does what good prose should do, which is to take you to places where you would not otherwise go and think about things afresh. You might not change your worldview, but grey is introduced into what was once black and white and old certainties no longer seem so certain. This remarkable book does that in volumes. The bulk of it was originally written in what is sometimes called automatic writing, where the author becomes a spiritual medium, taking dictation from an unseen hand that he or she has little control over.

I'm not a spiritual person. I have no mature thoughts about whether there is an afterlife or we just get a single bite of the cherry. I have a lot more in common with Doubting Thomas than the apostle who shares my name. I find the concept of pearly gates, heaven, a God with a white beard, and the rest of the stuff that most of our heads were filled with during our formative years amusing and, at times, oddly comforting. My younger brother Tim died recently. He was a musical genius. I always had a fantasy as a child that when he got to heaven, he would play piano duets with Mozart and Beethoven. It is a thought that has returned to me since his recent passing, embellished by visions of him introducing Mozart to the subtle virtues of modern dance music and much else that has happened musically during the last two centuries. Day dreamy thoughts of this nature are easier to have than thoughts that I'll never see him again.

In all seriousness, however, I feel a disquieting sense that odd things happen that cannot be accounted for in a rational way, which I suspect is true for a lot of people. It's not something I'm inclined to explore much, but I do admire people who go there, especially when it's not for personal gain. Dan Farish is such a person. To do so, he will have to overcome an understandable reluctance from some readers, knowing that some will judge anyone who writes about spirits and the way they interact with those of us in this world as someone that must have a screw loose.

I worked as a psychiatric nurse for a quarter of a century in a variety of settings, including mental hospitals, and can vouch for Dan's sanity. He is not psychotic and I should know. I can also vouch for his integrity and sincerity, which is why I take seriously anything he says or writes.

There is no question the text that follows is likely to be divisive. Some will dismiss it after a sentence or two, while others will find a topic they feel to be true written in a far better way than they could articulate themselves. Still others will pause, ponder and wonder about the way we humans are connected with the universe and with one another. I urge you to read this book and to do so with an open mind.

Peter Cross

Auckland, New Zealand 2012.

Part One

Living in the Afterlife

Chapter One

Introduction To The Spirit World

What if I told you that I know for a fact we never die when our bodies do and that there is life beyond what we see in this world? Would you believe me or would you say there is no way anyone could ever know what happens when we die?

If I told you that the spirit world shared the purpose of life with me and asked me to share it with you, would you doubt it? Would you brand me as a raving lunatic and/or a pathological liar? Or worse – might you have been told by church or society that anyone that claims to have received communications from the afterlife must be possessed by demons and is, therefore, guilty of black magic, blasphemy and heresy?

What if I shared some communications from the "other side" with you and explained how I got them?

Well, at the risk of being called crazy, or worse, I'm going to share some information that has been shared with me. Why? Because it might help someone out there that needs to understand there is far more to life than meets the eye.

In recent years, not one, but two very gifted spirit mediums informed me that I belong to a "soul group" consisting of seven writers (eight, including me) no longer living in the physical realm and that this soul group wanted me to write a book on their behalf. I'd never been much of a reader, let alone a writer, and the last time I'd written anything longer than a grocery list was thirty years earlier, which consisted of handing in a high school English class assignment.

One of these gifted mediums lives in New Zealand. The other lives in the Netherlands and the two have never met. Yet, both conveyed the same information about the seven writers, including the same names of two of the soul group members, Jacob and William. Yes, dead people apparently have actual names and some of them like to write. Not only do these two spirit mediums live on opposite sides of the world, neither had any more knowledge of me than they did about one another.

Like most people, I was more than a little skeptical about these communications from now deceased souls. My long-lost soul group members must have anticipated this, as they soon began communicating personal information that even the craftiest fake psychic and Scotland Yard together could never have known. The two mediums were able to contact a good number of departed souls that were once close to me in life.

Each of them shared deeply personal details about people or places of my past, including the names of a deceased friend's two sisters. Another close friend of mine, now passed over, came through with a long forgotten nickname of mine that only he called me. Still another departed loved one spoke of a hitching post in front of her childhood home that neither the medium nor I knew existed. That is, until I drove past her old house one day and saw an old hitching post staring back. My sister also popped in to say hello and mentioned childhood memories we shared that I've never told anyone on earth. She also wanted me to know that the addiction that killed her was a "dumb ass" thing to do and she was never going to do that again. The dumb ass wording caught my eye because it was one of her favorite expressions in life.

These are called "affirmations" and were given as a way to convince me that both the souls and the spiritual medium were the "real deal". It worked.

Over the course of several weeks, the souls shared their views on a variety of topics, ranging from romantic love vs. divine love, murder, abortion, capital punishment and other earthly issues. The bottom line, however, is a message they repeated many times over –

1. We arrive in *this* world to overcome obstacles we have chosen to accept before our arrival here. It's how we grow and learn to "Lighten Up" as souls.

2. Loving life and one another is the reason we are here. Learning to apply and share love in all we do is another way we grow as souls. Learning to apply faith is the key to living a fulfilling life.

They added that they want people in this world to understand life in their world and asked me to write a book explaining the afterlife to the best of my ability.

I protested that my writing experience was nil and I wouldn't know how to begin, but they assured me that I was the right man for the job and that Peter would help me. Have I mentioned Peter? Well, Peter was the writing tutor they told me I would meet in Auckland, New Zealand, at some point in the future. They didn't say when we would meet, but did say where he lived, including his street name and city. I was living in a tiny apartment above my sister's garage in Massachusetts at the time. They went on to describe Peter in detail, adding that he was a short man who wore eyeglasses and was born and raised in England. They said that he knew a lot about writing and he would help me pull the book together. I'd been planning on moving to New Zealand in the near future, but knew money would be tight when arriving, so put the book on the back burner and spent the next four years building my tile repair business. By the time I finally got around to writing a book, I'd completely forgotten about this man called Peter. After enrolling in an online writing course, I emailed the course instructor with a few questions. He suggested it would be easier to answer them in person. When we met a few days later, lo and behold, a short Englishman wearing spectacles walked up, shook my hand, and introduced himself as Peter. He was a brilliant tutor and we remain very close friends to this day.

Writing a book that would help people understand there is an afterlife is something I've been meaning to do since 2004, when the Seven Soul Writers passed their messages along. Eight years later, I finally feel somewhat qualified to deliver my end of the bargain, although I don't pretend to be an authority on the afterlife in any way. My only glimpse of life beyond this world resulted from an intense spiritual experience that instantly removed a 20-year addiction to alcohol in 1993. As a result of the experience, I wrote a book called ***Three Steps To Recovery*** two years ago, which is based on personal experience of connecting with a Higher Power than my own. It was an intense, amazing experience, which convinced me that there is more to life than we see in this world and that a power greater than our own not only exists, but consists of nothing but pure, divine love.

The experience was nothing short of a miracle and there are no words to describe it. One day, while wondering how to begin explaining to this world that invisible, dead people wanted me to tell their story, the idea hit me. The perfect vehicle to convey the spirit world's message and help people struggling with spiritual dis-ease – which is the true definition of addiction and many other issues – would be to write a book about the spiritual experience.

I have since learned that many of the ideas that suddenly pop into our thoughts are not actually of our own making and the unseen hands of others guided much of the writing in my first book. I fully expect to receive the same guidance while writing this one. The souls call this "pouring oil", meaning they use the spiritual connection between themselves and the person they watch over to instill knowledge and love. They refer to this spiritual connection as "wires" consisting of love.

The wires act much like a telephone line, allowing two parties to communicate.

You will learn other unusual words and terms in this book, as well, like Wings and Lumes and Unlit Souls. You will read the Seven Souls' views of life in their world, as well as this one. I've done my best to act as the messenger for the souls without adding my own opinions and beliefs. It should be fairly easy to differentiate their writing style from mine. They write much the same way they spoke a century or two ago, when they last walked in this world. When you see words like "hooey" or "woggle" or "wax and wane", I guarantee they didn't come from me. I've also *italicized* my own words, except in the final chapter, which you will read as chapter introductions.

To give you an idea of the way people spoke a century or more ago, here is an example of how one of the Seven Writers speaks –

"When we come to you we are like we once were in the world, because we must dress ourselves in the images of the past to communicate with you. This is why we can talk with you in a human way. We wish to be clear why we find it so difficult to write these words. It is because speech has changed since we were last on earth. It was a whole lifetime ago for me and even longer for others of us. What will Danny say if I tell him he is john with a writer's cap? That means he is john other. John means clever, other means other than usual. I am Jack from Wales. Wales was where I lived when I last was on earth."

They got the "other" part correct, at least.

Chapter One - Introduction To The Spirit World

Chapter Two

Meet The 7 Writers

In 2004, the spirit medium I had recently met explained that there was a group of spirit writers wanting to know if I would like to "meet" them. The first answer to cross my mind was a resounding no. I was in no hurry to get too close to their world, if you know what I mean. Once the medium assured me that the meeting would take place on paper only and the grim reaper wasn't calling my name just yet, I agreed to hear them out. This is what they had to say.

There is a long tale to tell. Have you the time? There is a

plan here in our world, just as there is in yours. Our plan is to work in love because we are love. We are no longer people, as we once were. To us, love is the only thing. There is nothing else. Love greater than life is where we live now. This love houses life. There is no other focus for us. Overall, the things we do are witnesses to love in all its guises. We give love because it isn't an option for us to do anything else. It is our nature to give, yes.

We want people to know that life on earth is their "job" and that arriving here in this place is like leaving work. There are so many who want to know about the afterlife, but too many viewpoints are open about the subject. When this book is written it will be in our words, and what better than straight from the horse's mouth?

Things here are very different than in the physical world. Firstly, there is nothing material in this place. Although nothing physical exists here, one could say there are still worlds within worlds. There are areas devoted to different things. It is important to remember that there is nothing man can do without the support of love. You must never forget it. The minds and bodies of men are just that; the thoughts and experiences they carry do no lasting harm to the soul, after all.

War is an enemy of people, but not of love or the immortal soul. Whether you die by old age or by the gun, you still find light, love and joy when you arrive in the afterlife. People imagine that dying young or violently are terrible events, but they are not at all for those that arrive here. Love conquers all, as they say, and it is true. The newly deceased soul doesn't bemoan his fate, no matter how he or she died. Only human souls do that. This is what we most want people to understand about dying... that death, in whatever form it takes, is perfectly natural, no matter what age you are when you die. Death is a consequence of living. Life may be beautiful or horror filled, but it just a thing. It is an adventure of the soul. The body dies, but the soul lives always. Not only does the soul live on, but dwells in a perfect state of love here in our world.

There is so much this book will give to people. It is a hate-filled world for some. Many people have given up on giving, have hidden their hearts, and have quit trying to love one another. People live in the belief that they must be tough minded and hard hearted in order to survive. With our book to walk them though all of it, there will be an opening into which love will flow. What we give you is not the last testament, nor our bias or personal opinions. This book is about the life that you will all enter into one day simply by tripping over it. We want people to walk with the awareness that life is like a trip to an amusement park. There are the scary rides full of ups and downs, as well as the fun prizes.

Without all the trappings that come with a physical body and all the heavy load of earthly living, love is a simple thing. *So* simple that it is easily overlooked while living with the harsh realities of the mortal world. No one waits to die, but plenty wait to begin living. The haves and have-nots mean nothing in the face of eternal life. The cold and the heat of a day might affect your bodies, but never affect the soul. The heartbreak of love and the pain of illness are soon forgotten when the soul leaves the body. There is one great leveler in all this living and that is love. Living in a pure, unconditional state of love changes everything. The afterlife is so much fuller than the empty room of worldly possessions and self-protection that so many experience in mortal life.

Love is all you need, just as the song says. You might lack money or food on the table, but if you use your faith to turn a frown into a smile, it is much easier to bear and assists love in the way it gives to you. Those that expect to receive love without joining forces with it offer nothing to the world, really, and the things they hope for feel empty when received. There is no such thing as a hopeless love. There are hopeless lives, however, and hollow living runs against the very nature of life itself. The lessons we learn here in the place of light and love, which we now share with you, are that taking from the world only acquires possessions. Unless we learn to give, as well, taking is a soulless act.

Mark this as our arrival. We declare ourselves as Seven Wings who write these words for you. We are wording this book with you in mind, using these writings as a testament to our existence. Always listening, we agree that it is a sincere effort we all make together in writing this book.

Rings are binding tokens of love and we pledge you our ring. The band is made of love and there are seven white gems that give light. Two are white gold, one is white light, endlessly, and four are white violet.

In this group, there is myself, Mary, along with Jake, Bill, three other men, and a lady who gives the love we use to write these words. She is the white woman. The seventh man is not always here. He comes and goes. His job is not to actually write the book, but to direct the writing. We trust one another to write if we are not all present at the same time. This is because our direction is planned ahead of time. We govern (guide) in this way to inform you and also to love you. It is one thing to simply give you knowledge, but it is useless unless you have the love of God to help you to fully understand the knowledge we give you.

Mary Hastons is one of us. Mary was very well to do in life and she walked over Bunker Hill while Paul Revere journeyed with his lanterns. Mary lived well and had no opinion of the Brits. She is entombed in Ploughman's Field, which was located in Boston, but has now become a land covered by many buildings.

There is Bill, who is Danny's uncle in this place, but was not in life. He is Danny's grandmother's companion in this place and lived before Danny was born. He is originally from Johnstown. Bill had a serious drinking problem in life, but now watches over Danny as his favorite pastime.

Another of us is named John. He likes to tell you he wakes up the living, as opposed to waking the dead. He is usually only a bystander most of the time and writes only occasionally, but he is part of the team.

A Native American is also part of the group. Although he has written nothing for the book, his interest was in watching the process. The book is flowing aloud here and he comes to listen. He is just an observer, so he is not one of the writers. He is in this because he once watched over plodding (struggling) Danny. Now Danny is free to go out and give to the world. He still looks on, though.

There is Jack from Wales. He can't be called into writing too often, as his opinion is too Godly even for us, and he interprets things through his own beliefs. Old ideas die hard, yet his views are important, too, because he is an old soul here and old souls knows all sides of many things.

There is a white woman, as well, but she is not a Wing (messenger, light worker) like us. She is a Lume (illuminated higher level soul) and she never says anything at all. She is off and on in her appearance because Lumes never stay still in this place. She has no name that we call her by, as she is enlightened beyond human names. Her role in the book is to make sure we give to it obediently, without overlooking anything, and without elaborating from our own personal point of view.

Danny's best friend in life, Ricky, came and went when we began writing, but he stayed more often towards the end because he became more and more interested in the whole idea of passing on information in this way. He liked the idea of helping his pal write a book from beginning to end and he is an active participant in all our communications.

Jacob is one of the writers, but he is rarely called by that name here. It was his earthly name, but most of us go by our middle names or even other names here and he is known as

James in this place. James is simply one of the seven writers who believe that this book can give something positive to the world.

We write these words without the bias that religion or new age ideas carry with their message. The purpose of our communication is to bridge the gap between man and life everlasting. It is our hope that earthly souls will receive a little ease and refreshment in how they view life, so that they will be able to live with less fear and give to life all that it deserves... which is all the love you are able to give, be it in your thoughts, your actions, or simply believing that there is more to life than any one religion can teach you.

We writers have come together because it is our mutual purpose to send our words to the world through you.

The joy of being alive here is beyond pleasure... beyond imagination. It is like the whole falling of one's stomach and becoming as one with a beautiful song. Life here is deeply and wondrously joyful. There is the huge freedom of non-constraint that comes with the heaviness of earthly living. Our bodies are made of pure light and dash about without movement or effort of any kind. All we have to do is think of a place and in a twinkle we are where we want to be.

No words can describe the knowing we feel in light or the flood of love that carries us through each illusion of others. To say that we look like angels is actually an old, inaccurate image. Really, we look illuminated by light. Visions of light dancing on water fill my thoughts while describing it. We appear in human form sometimes. At other times, we appear like eggs (orbs) of light. We have become ovals of ethereal faces altered by love, no longer feeling tired or showing the wrinkles and lines we wore in human life.

Light irons out all blemishes that life created. Robes are what angels wear in man's images of us, but we have no robes.

We are just light and pure love streams from us. We appear to each other like the softest glow of light or the most dazzling flares. There is no way to describe the difference between earthly life and ours, except to say that one day you will give yourself to it with the same awe and delight as we did. We live on in this place of love forever, in one way or another, be it life here or returning to life on earth. There are ways to live in our world that are given to us all, whether we are wholly or partly enlightened.

Chapter Three

Science Of Love

How Souls Cross Between Two Worlds

The souls assure us that we all consist of just two things once our soul leaves our physical body and crosses over to the other side of life - light and love. While I have no reason to doubt them, science was not one of my better school subjects and I struggled with the concept of love as a form of molecular energy for some time after reading their description. It was only when I recalled the spiritual experience that healed my addiction that it began to make sense. I'd been "zapped" (for lack of a better word) with waves of pure love and warmth beyond description. The energy was extremely intense, yet exhilarating and calming, as well.

After struggling with concepts like spaces between atoms and the Big Bang theory for a while - and feeling somewhat frustrated - I asked the medium to ask the souls how they would explain love to a child. This was their reply, which I suspect was written with my science-challenged brain in mind. Their explanation reminded me not to apply for a job with N.A.S.A. anytime soon.

"If I were to explain love to a child, Danny, I would say life is full of light sparkles that make everything beautiful. Everything sparkles, and when we are very kind and do our very best, we sparkle, too. That is what I would tell a child about love."

Left to himself without love to guide him, man would have no common link to join with others. There would be no pairing off of kindred spirits. There would be no sense of order or society in the world.

Love is the most basic element in the make-up of the universe. The love and light we speak of throughout this book define the life that fills all living things to some degree. Light is the spacing between atoms. Quite simply love **is** the atoms. An atom could not organize itself into forming anything, however, without the sound of light. The sound of light has been recorded, but isn't recognized for what it really is. It is a love that exists even within the absence of known life. Time itself is light made of love because, again, without love there would be no order.

This may be hard to imagine and yet it is so. Where is this light located? We say it is everywhere and can be seen in all things, even in the darkest shade of black. Color, even black, is just another organized system, after all. Color responds to certain laws and is oblivious to anything but itself and the exertion of itself. Love is the essence of all creation, which is found in all things and creatures, be it a newborn baby, the tiniest insect, a pebble or a tree. Light is the carrier of love. Much like a computer cable carries information, light carries love.

So we say that light/love is the very basis of anything you can think of. It is the source of all existence and it is the essence of creation. While it did not build the world as a single-minded creation, love made it possible for the world to create itself and to rule itself according to the light.

That is why we say the world exists in, and of, itself... meaning that it exists because of love, but love did not purposely create it. The life upon the earth and the moon that orbits around it are obedient to the organizing effect of light, as are the stars that shine above it. There is nothing in existence that is not a carrier of love and light.

Mankind has always been the very embodiment of love, even from the beginning, and lives only because of it. God is another name for love, but we prefer to use the two words, love and light, to describe different parts of love.

Love is the substance of life. God is the whole entity that our love has built God up to be. God is love and light. As an actual entity, God doesn't exist. As a belief, however, he does. So "God" has a life because of it, just as any deity assumes a kind of life when prayer and projected faith and illusion are built up. While there seems to be no God reality, he is a belief... but a belief that has a presence. Yes, all those Gods that the world has worshiped over the eons do have an existence. Their existence is limited to man's beliefs, but it is there all the same. God, as man envisions it, cannot change anything. He is a belief, not a basic element of life.

Love can't walk by itself. It can't endure in a vacuum, either, which is why it started in the first place. There was always love and physical reality. The Big Bang that science speaks of still needed something to blow apart, didn't it? While we talk of love as a beneficial and joyous thing, it is a real thing that illuminates all. Like any illumination, it has joy and comfort at its heart. Love is a simple system that promotes and sustains the fabric of life.

When our body dies our soul is released to rejoin love's system of never ending life. We work in love, here in our world, to maintain it. We work tirelessly and endlessly to keep love growing. Which, in turn, allows love to experience even greater levels of love. We could not do anything other than work for love and light because we are made of it. As humans, you carry love at the inner core of your every cell. When your physical body dies the love inside you is released from your body to rejoin with love. Like popping a balloon causes the air inside to fly back into the atmosphere and rejoin with it, the love within us does the same. Our soul, our essence, rejoins its own kind.

Love inhabits your body and shapes it in many ways. Since love is an organizing force, it assembles itself in its memory of a person. The things that affected you personally in life, both positive and negative, shape the soul within you. Any experiences that threaten a person's love are actions that threaten love's existence and also create wounds of the psyche/soul. So, the soul releases from the body with the memory of the person it inhabited intact. The soul contains memories of the person's physical state.

Chapter Four

Types Of Souls

This chapter discusses the two basic types of souls humans possess, as well as a third type of human. According to the Wings, some humans are born with no soul at all. The Wings suggest this type is little more than an animal. Along with their claims that there is no God (as people know it), the idea that soulless men walk amongst us is bound to challenge some readers' beliefs. Come to think of it, challenging man's beliefs just might be the point of this book. Anyhow, if anyone feels offended, please take the matter up with the Wings.

Types Of Souls

Wings

Today we will talk about Wings. This is about Wings as a whole. In order to explain this type of soul, we must tell you about the love that creates them. Wings living in the world haven't any superior knowledge or advantage over other types of souls. Being born into the physical world cripples any essential knowledge that Wings may possess.

What Wings do have, though, is a sense of purpose. They are usually beyond themselves and are able to rise above their circumstances. They come to earth on a mission, not a whim, and they know inside that there is light at the end of the tunnel. For a man, it is worthwhile to know that life is not against him. Love is not a test of strength, but is really him walking hand in hand with love. Many Wings do not work out their missions in a few years. Some even leave the world as so-called victims and leave their example for others to learn and grow from. Many live without achieving anything at all, except the love of their families. Being alive in the world is important, even without completing missions, because a Wing always brings love with him as a way to enrich the lives of others.

Are all people Wings?

The world and the people in it are a part of love, as love is invested into every part of life. Yet, like any investment, there is more energy given to some parts than others. When Wings wave (make their presence felt) it is noticeable to both other humans and spirits. They wave from their need for love. At other times, they hasten towards an event that fills them with excitement.

Wings wave like a dog wags its tail (wagging), in the same way exactly. This indicates to all that a Wing has a high rate of vibration (wobbling) that waits for an issue, be it in receiving love or assisting with an upcoming event, such as a birth or death. Wings hover over the people they shared love with in life and it is the way they Lighten Up. Just by basking in them I am able to view their life and be with them in love. In my case, the people closest to me in life are over my leaving now. During my younger years I had a major drinking problem and my actions left wounds on some people. I crossed over years ago and my loved ones have grown older as I hover above them. I have given up habits they wasted words on me with in life and today I am used as an example of what not to do.

I wasted many years of my life drinking and womanizing. I know now that they were ways to be avoided. I wasn't very jolly at the end. Of course, I never knew the whole story then. The issues given to me in life were presented as opportunities to learn and grow as a soul. God ensures life is tough at times as a way to enable us to learn how to love with compassion and understanding. How can we achieve light within if we have no issues to spark our understanding? The lessons we are given are always about love, even when there is little evidence of it.

A Wing's sojourn on earth is not rated in any way by success or failure. It is always loving and worth the trip. If you demonstrate how to rise above your pre-destined wounds, you help create love in the world. You learn to express love in all its shapes and forms, such as respect, affection, trust, and commitment. All the finest of human qualities roll on from a Wing demonstrating his or her power to live in faith and love.

Unlit Souls

All souls have love, but not all have light. Some are souls that make it up here and just look on. Others will eventually surrender to love and learn to Lighten Up, but Wings always go to the light. Quite simply, some souls are given life, but are not from the light of love. These ones cause trouble in the world, but are still loved in this place.

They can't grow in light, but can be loved and they look on forever in a love of their own. Unlit souls have auras, as do all living things. But, at the same time, they are without the spark of love within them that lights a Wing. Although they are without the light of love, all souls are still loved in this place. There is no definition of bad or evil here.

There are Unlit Souls and there are Wings. It is enough to know that light is the love of all things. This day we will talk about living in love.

To live is easy. The human body is a machine, of sorts, and the machine works well in long-term living. The way you live is up to you. This is called free will. While the roles we play in life are set from the beginning, change is always an option. The child born into a warm and loving home usually grows into a warm and loving adult. The reverse is also true for the child raised in a harsh environment. We normally begin making choices while we are still children. We adopt some things or turn away from them. Wounded children discover fear and doubt. Happy kids find joy in achievement and giving to life by being a part of it. Yet, even the happiest home can breed a wayward child, while a troubled child can become a good adult. This is due to both the make-up of the child and the governing (guidance) given by his caretakers.

Imagine being born into a family that was without love. This child might well live and die as his parents did, without joy and hope. Yet, some children learn to feel joy despite the harshness they have experienced and go on to live happily as adults. There are some people who shine in their environments, whether it is a harsh or loving environment. This is because their life has not been lived in a machine mode, but was a life lived joyfully. Joyfully, as in relishing everything. Seeing the light when they look up to the sky, rather than just the clouds. There is hope inside them that takes them outside of their square box and it is their faith that life is to be lived happily that marks them as exceptional. By choosing to live in faith, they have marked their wings with light, vivid colors. They are the colors of love. Many Wings choose to be born into loveless families in order to spread love to others.

These people often tend to die younger than others because the light, love, and faith within them gives all of itself to others. In other words, the brighter one shines, the harder it becomes to remain earthbound. They are literally Lightening Up, both physically and spiritually. The way they die isn't important, whether it be from illness or by the bullet. They just have to leave earth once they have completed their life mission. Love cares not about assisting bodies, but souls.

The thing that allows man to become more than just a body is in the variety of ways men are created. Just as you find many different leaves on a tree, they are all still leaves. Some are more full and vibrant than others. Man is the same. He is created by love, initially, and possesses a spark of this love within him. Some people have more space within them for this spark than others, quite simply, and that is the difference between a Wing and other men. Wings are not Angels, nor God's helpers, in that sense. They exist simply because their ego is smaller and light is larger. Wings hold more light than other people. Man comes in many varieties, depending upon his cellular structure, and it is the luck of the draw as to a person's make up. By this, we aren't talking only about a person's genetic make up, but simply the way that light flows though a person. A Wing has more love and light energy flowing through him than an unlit soul. Even the unlit people of the world are all a part of a whole. It isn't through their own fault that less light flows through them than it does through others. That is the reason all souls are loved equally.

Should an unlit soul be given the opportunity to return to the world again, there is an even chance that he might become a Wing when he is re-born into a human body. So, you see, we can say we are all God's children. There is no difference. We are all a part of love.

Also, an unlit soul is never denied love's light when he or she arrives here in our world. An unlit person often does harmful things in his worldly life because he has no light passing through him. Again, this is not his or her fault. As we have said, it is just the luck of the draw. Even though causing harm to others is heartbreaking to most people, it is part of life in the world. Unlit souls cannot be changed in earthly life and that is why laws are written to keep them out of man's society. Although their wrongdoing goes against man's view of life, their actions do not present a danger to life itself. Life is eternal and both the unlit soul and their victim returns here upon death, as do all souls. The force of life, which is love, is far greater than any mortal can imagine in his wildest dreams. Even if man were to completely destroy his world, life would still return to love and love entirely devotes itself to creating more life. Blowing up the world would certainly destroy "life as you know it", but life would continue, regardless.

Imagine life as a giant bonfire.... all consuming and bright, with sparks flying upwards and into the night. The energy that creates the spark rises up to meet the air that feeds the fire. Some sparks become part of the air they rise to meet, while some fall to the ground and start yet another bonfire. It matters not, however, as the fire it creates will generate even more sparks and the cycle continues. All the air that fuels the spark becomes one again with the air eventually. Whether as a beautiful spark rising in the night air or a fallen spark that ignites more fire, all sparks naturally seek air. So, no matter how many fires are ignited, there will always be more sparks rising to feed from its catalyst, which is air.

Wings return to earth not out of a desire to live as a human, but return out of a desire to become one with love... to become one with the light. It is an ambition born within Wings because love is all we desire and love cannot help but re-create itself, always.

Soulless Men

Contrary to popular belief, all men are not created equal and not every human has a soul. To have wings is to have a soul, yet not every soul has wings. There will always be men without souls. Some men are born with little more than their bodies. They are very often hard people that do much damage in the world by their lack of giving. The soulless often wind up in jail and spend their lives wounding others with their disregard of life and love.

How can people have no soul?

Cast your mind to Nazi Germany. The party leader was a soulless person, born of a woman that was also without a soul. Just like any inheritance, some people come from a long line of soulless births. They are to be accepted as being the same as others, just as a person with red hair is accepted in a blonde family. They are still family, but different. They have no reason to live, other than to exist and do as they will, not as society or love would have them do. They are not devils or descendants of evildoers. They are simply born that way, like offspring born with a genetic defect. While these people seldom, if ever, live beneficial lives, they do exist because of love. As a result, they have the same right to be in the world as any other creature.

As Wings, we live many lives throughout eternity, going back to earth time and time again to assist one of our own soul group members and to give love to all. We cannot refuse to love anyone if we want to be as we should. If it means loving a soulless person, then we do love him or her. It gives them love, which has its value, since most of them have been deprived of love in their lives and have little hope of ever knowing love in a normal way. They are not evil. They just lack the soul needed to give love and the ground is where they stay on their departure from life. Having told you this, I will also say that love also creates wisdom and wisdom improves the lives of all that it touches.

Lumes

After many, many incarnations a soul Lightens Up to such a level that human issues no longer concern them. A Wing can stay here, in this place, or return to earth as a mortal. It's the soul's choice, but returning to mortal life ensures further Lightening Up. If one chooses to view life as an organization, rather than from a narrower point of view, then he can understand that there is a structure to life. This nature of this structure is to progress and create love. Love is its only purpose.

The higher-ups in the tiers of light also have soul groups,

as do we Wings beneath them. These higher-ups are called Lumes. But they are concerned with the forces of life itself, in other places, and attend to the prosperity of life on other levels. These souls are so unearthly in their existence that they will never make contact with the world. Earth is but a small thing in the sum of love.

Chapter Five

Soul Groups and Reincarnation

I've tried not to interfere too much with the souls'
messages of this book. Apart from adding the occasional
translation of the souls' antiquated words into modern
day English - like defining "toggle" (to change from one
state to another), for example, this book was written
entirely by the Seven Souls and the spiritual medium
via "automatic writing". The medium holds the pen to
paper and the souls do the rest. As you read through this

chapter, however, you'll learn about a visit my deceased best friend, Ricky, paid me one night a number of years ago. Ricky was neither transparent nor solid when he appeared. He was translucent, meaning he was not at all solid, yet his facial features and body shape were clearly defined. The entire room filled with a warmth and love I have never felt before or since that night. Although Ricky appeared to me in the early 90's, time not only stood still, but also turned back to the time we'd spent together in the 70's. It was as if the twenty plus years between his appearance and the day we'd last spoken had never passed.

Yesterday, we discussed types of souls.

Today we will talk about soul groups.

Wings in the afterlife assist Wings living in the world. Wings also return to earth from this place to live mortal lives, if they choose, although it is not a requirement.

The Wing is born or re-born into the world to carry love to others. He arrives with a mission. Although he carries a purpose, the given odds are low of achieving it because there are so many ways he can be diverted from it in the world. For the most part, the mission is a small one. It may just be to be with his soul group members on earth and to support them in their joint desire to live out their lives.

A Wing descends to earth as a newborn. He comes because of a call from one of his soul group members on earth and he arrives to assist that soul in living out love or to address a loved one's issue. In descending, he takes on the clothing of his soul, along with his earthly inheritance, such as family and the world's situation at the time. To take on physical form is to take on an ego and, like most Wings, he or she will be clever in his particular way. There are few Wings that return to earth without the wits to support the wisdom buried within them. The Wing has a gift of some sort. The person might be musically talented, for example. It is usually a communications gift, such as writing or talking. Using this gift is how wisdom can be spread to others.

There is also a wound (emotional pain/trauma) to take on, as well, and the reason for this is to communicate this wisdom in human form. It is a means to communicate with our kind and with the world. Call it a trump card. The Wing can use the wound as a way to show the world that man has the ability to rise above himself and his problems in life, whether they are internal or external problems. The earthbound Wing has no conscious knowledge of the wound (emotional or physical) he or she has agreed to carry before arriving in the world, of course. Nor is the person aware of the reason they are given a communication or other special gift to share with others.

With others in his soul group, he can give much to the world and to one another. Waves of love are evident when soul group members reunite on earth. Watching souls coving (circling/gathering) together is a beautiful sight to observe. Hovering is how we see this from above and it is one of the ways we observe human lives. But we concentrate only on a few souls, so we can apply loving to them alone. We work in this way because we have loved these people, either in this place or in worldly life, and have an attachment with them. We also lay over them to help iron out the wounds of those we love. We help to heal scars on the psyche of people in order to keep their love intact and to ease their way for when they return here. It is done out of love... for the protection and sake of love itself.

This is the entire thing that we are as Wings. Some of our soul group members exist in human form and we protect their souls as best we can. This means that even while your human life might be struggling at times, your soul is intact and enclosed within our pure loving touch. For us, "our love" means our soul groups. They are like family and they are lights we have an attachment with by the love of God. We call these attachments "wires" that are made of love and light.

Members of the same soul group descend to be born into their own group. Not necessarily in the same group as the families into which they are born. One soul group, for instance, might be concerned with justice in the world, or the lack of it. Another group might consist of preachers and arrive in the world to spread the word of light and love. To say that they only come back as lawyers or preachers, however, would be silly. Wings also take on worldly life in order to develop the less enlightened souls. They come back in any lifestyle, but all members of that particular soul group share the same "mission", which is to spread love. Some Wings might come to earth as a homeless person in order to to assist other homeless people or to make the world aware of their plight. Another Wing might serve time in prison to help other inmates, either directly or indirectly. One thing is certain about Wings, though, and that is a Wing can never commit murder. No soul is ever sent back to earth to learn justice or other lessons in that way, although he might land in a court of law for other reasons.

Wings create other Wings by living in the world and working love. Tangled wires (people struggling) give us the opportunity to descend and lay over troubled souls. Though all souls have their place here in the afterlife, it is finer for them to be enlightened in love. The more we work love, the more love grows and the greater the life the whole world will know.

In the world of man there is no life that does not have importance or a love to call its own. Everyone is given love to attach him to emotional love within families and within his created groups of friends, partners, and children. We Wings can love within these groups. We install ourselves within these groups and use our worldly lives as examples of the grace of living and loving and dying. By being part of a human group, we make links to others, allowing them the water of love needed to grow their wings.

When Danny was in despair, he had the love of his friend, Ricky, to lighten him up. For Ricky to display himself required an act of great love and will. Ricky's mission was hoping for love's sake that he would be seen and recognized by Danny. People think that if they pray to God they will be answered in some way. But love isn't about an answer to a prayer, really. Love is an actual living thing that can be used and given. When we take on human form our appearance has marked effects on people and takes them outside of themselves. This opens them to look towards life after death without fear. The reason Ricky was able to appear to Danny was because of the "wires" of love that connect them as souls. It was Danny's heavy emotional state that not only alerted Ricky to the situation, but also allowed him to descend to be with Danny. He was literally "taking on the weight" of his best friend's energy at the time.

One purpose of a Wing's soul is to dwell within the body and woggle (engage) with other members of his or her soul group. Interacting with other soul group members gives him a sense of happiness and blessing. It is the joy people feel in the company of another. Another purpose of a Wing's soul is to allow a Wing to connect with and comfort an earthbound soul group member in times of trouble, as Ricky did with Danny.

Each Wing is part of a tier in our world here. A tier is similar to a stage of enlightenment one has reached. There are different levels we move through as we Lighten Up. The more we Lighten Up, the more we work at a distance between the world and us. When we have reached a certain level we are no longer concerned with working love for humans, viewing instead more defined ways to use light.

A soul group's members tend to keep pace with one another, allowing for assistance from others in the group, if called upon. There are members of the group both here and on earth, as well. There is no set limit to a group. A group's numbers can be in the millions. Each group is loving towards the other group members in this way. No one stays eternally poor or eternally rich when returning to life on earth. Everyone has their turn in life, as the saying goes. The groups work in this way because to know life is to know all things. It is a way to learn all the colors of experience. Once a soul group has concerned itself with an issue, the group will continue working it, going back to earth as many times as it likes. Eventually there is one love that is so filling for a Wing that the soul becomes lighter. The Wing then ascends a little lighter and higher into another group with a different center of focus.

After many lifetimes there is no color remaining in the soul's wings. They become a pure white sheet of flaming light.

Chapter Six

The Viewing And Illusion

Earlier, the Wings discussed terms like woggle and wires and unlit souls. This chapter explains the viewing new souls receive when they first cross over to the afterlife. There's the "welcoming committee", which consists of the person's soul group members. Their job is to greet the new arrival in the afterlife and present the new soul with a "viewing" (review) of his or her mortal life. Then there is the "illusion" given to the new arrival, which truly is heavenly in its nature. The new soul becomes suspended in the happiest moments of his or her life, which eases the shock of arriving in the afterlife and dulls the pain of the "wounds" he or she suffered and caused others in life. The viewing and illusion are tools that allow the newly arrived soul to see precisely how he did or did not live his life. This is not done as punishment. Nor is the viewing given to judge his "sins", as neither of those things exists in the next life. They are given in order to help the person learn the true meaning of life, which is to live in an eternal state of love and joy. The new soul is gradually "loved up" from his illusion and the next step begins the endless, beautiful process of "Lightening Up". Here is how they explain it.

As much as people would like to think they'll be drifting around in white robes sipping tea or meeting a famous rock star when they cross over, the truth is that they will be joyfully filling themselves with pure love and light and feel no curiosity, nor need, to socialize with anyone. People also imagine they will be reunited with all their loved ones and live happily ever after in some eternal domestic bliss. This also doesn't happen. Those that have looked over and loved the new soul arriving here are the ones that greet him, even if he never knew these people in earthly life. Each and every soul has others that care for him. Wings are like guardian angels, in the sense that they use love to guide and assist people. But, we seldom can, or would, intervene in a person's life. That is because each life is your own to live. It is yours to use or abuse as you like and whatever happens in life, you will return to love, regardless. So, a guardian angel or over looker cares for and comforts those he or she loves to the best of their ability by working love. We do this by soothing mortals living in the world, not by arranging events for them. Remember also that souls often have a mission to accomplish in life, if possible. It is pre-ordained in those cases and is not to be interfered with by us here, as love has already planned things out wisely ahead of time.

Upon arriving here, we give the soul his or her viewing. Not only does this viewing allow us to bond in love with this person, it's also a way to dissolve the painful memories he or she holds within their soul. Traumatic events, which we call wounds, leave their mark on the person's soul in life and this is why people are given illusions to help the soul heal. The illusion helps them to forget and release negative memories.

When a new soul arrives here, he is automatically detached from all things human, even in the case of a sudden or violent death. As he grows in light, the "forgetting" of pain and suffering he once knew is as effortless as the process of recording memories had been in his worldly life. Because there is no longer a need to strive for physical survival, there is no need for his brain to record anything new. He no longer has a body or a brain, of course. That isn't to say he doesn't arrive here with old memories intact, only that they are no longer important to him. In fact, he is given a viewing of his earthly life when he arrives so that the healing process, or

"Lightening Up" of his soul can soon begin. Before the process can begin, however, the new soul receives the viewing.

There he is, this new soul. Whether young or elderly, loved or unloved in the world, he has arrived to this place far beyond the reach of the life he once knew. He is now freer than anything he's ever known. It is an understatement to say he loves what he sees here. When he receives the viewing he begins to understand how he gave in life, or how he took from it. This is the first step in the healing process and it is a shock for every new soul. "This is how I really was in life?" he asks. He sees how unimportant all the material things he strived for in life really were, when all was said and done. He is also surprised to learn that, although he has given up worldly life, he feels more alive than ever before here in this place. He is more alive than even in his wildest dreams and this is because he now realizes the entire purpose of living is to spread love in its purest form. On earth, his attempts to love wisely are just shadows cast in a much greater light. It is simply wonderful for him to experience and there is no way to describe the look on a new soul's face as he realizes the true meaning of pure and total love.

He adores his new way of loving life and he no longer has any physical needs to worry or concern him. Placed here, he is also aware of those that mourn him. It is like your nightly dreams, where you recognize faces and scenes without being able, nor forced, to awaken from the dream. He sees his previous life on earth as a dream and that's why voices and faces are familiar, but are no longer important to him. He is already entering into the illusion he is being given, which is all he needs to fulfill the love he needs. All else is less than that, regardless of how much or little love he felt on earth. He sees and delves into many peoples' images of him. Man usually carries kindly images of a departed soul, but not all are so fond of him. He sees images and he sees the reason he is being given the illusion, which is to help him heal from his worldly wounds and to nurture his love.

The illusion he receives is of a more innocent time in his physical life, before he learned the cold cut of mastering his world. The illusion is of a time when he felt most loved. It was a time he felt most connected to love beyond any doubt. The images his mourners see of him float up and surround this new soul, attached to him by the "wires" of all those he affected in life. They are nebulous to him... changing and unreal, yet insistent and constant at first. The love with which he's now a part calms him, however, and so he faces the ugly and the sad with equal detachment. Strong, negative images can grow very thick, however, and they pull and weigh him downward as they become more tangible. This is why excessive grief or mourning holds a new soul back as he tries to Lighten Up. Although his wings have become white now that he lives in a state of pure love, these negative images mark his wings with the colors of bleeding love. They are the colors of the sadness, hurt, and mourning he created for others in his life. The people that think harshly of him or grieve him pull him downward, while at the same time, the illusion that feeds his love lifts him. Like a balloon, he rises and is pulled down again. Up and down, over and over. This is known as "wobbling" in this place.

If people think kindly of him, they add to his life by helping him heal in his illusion. Think of the way he wounded or hurt you, though, and you pull him down, filling his wings with the weight of things which no longer carry any consequence to him. Remember, there is no judgment or punishment here. Therefore, he is not wailing about his wrongdoings in a previous life. He is simply healing from the wounds he suffered in life that caused his wrongdoings in the first place. Imagine if I were to watch you and always thought only of a moment in your life when you were at your worst behavior. You would then be half light and half dark, held in place by my thoughts. The new soul is given his illusion to see him through until heavy thoughts such as grieving or anger have passed. All things must pass, as it is said, and all the souls he knew in life will also pass on and become one with the light, no matter how long it takes to happen. Peoples' images of us don't force us to look at our sins or errors in life, as those mean nothing here. By pulling us down, we are tinted with their dark colors (heavy emotions), but the light of love bleaches out those colors in time, until finally we are so healed and full of light we become color resistant.

A new soul can stay in his illusion for eons, if necessary. You might think of men that create war and kill millions, for example, and wonder if they ever heal. We guide souls through wounds of many types and degrees and this type of soul will hang onto their illusions longer than we will be here to guide them, as we also continue to Lighten Up. White is white and if there is no white present within a soul, there is no way it can become white. Others have souls, but they do not contain white. These souls will always remain in the illusion we give them and will never lighten up any further. We are talking about unlit souls, of course. Soulless men cannot return to a source from which they were never born and there is no place for them here.

White wings are given to the new Wing arriving here in order to heal the wounds he received in life. There is no love stronger than white light, so none of the murky colors of the world can ever mark us again, once we Lighten Up. We are touched by these colors as new arrivals here, but loved out of them as we Lighten Up. As they begin to forget themselves as humans, the love they carry within their soul is freed to rejoin itself in pure light. The soul begins to Lighten Up and the process continues until the memories of that soul are erased and love can work itself again. This gradually and slowly removes the state of illusion and also allows the new soul to look over those he or she has wronged in life. We review our earthly lives to understand that we were also wounded in life and how our wounds affected others. We then come to see the source of our wounds. We learn the reasons why love was clouded within us and why we passed on the hurt we felt to others. The viewing (or reviewing) of mortal life by a new soul arriving here is just one part of learning how to free ourselves from old wounds.

We can't change the harm done to us in earthly life, nor can we undo the harm we have caused others. The more a person works to Lighten Up during mortal life, the easier it will be for him to Lighten Up when he or she arrives here. We watch over humans in order to achieve an understanding of how life organizes itself in its outcomes. In doing so, we learn to better understand the importance of applying love. This is when we learn to look at colors, people, and how to best give them love. This is how the new soul learns and begins to unlearn all that is harmful to love.

People have come to give less love to one another and that is why there is more evidence of harsh, unloving behavior in today's world. Love, however, knows only love and there is no judgment or punishment handed out here in the light. We repeat these words throughout this book because it's important for people to understand. As a soul, you are always free to receive pure love. Nothing else exists here but light and love.

There is nothing given during the illusion that is harmful. There is no need because all souls thirst for love, and therefore all the illusions they dwell in are entirely about love. They might be given images of the love they knew as a baby or a young child, for example. Or live again as a teenager or perhaps flash back to a time when they settled into a warm, married life. The illusion given to them nurtures the seed of love within them and recreates the joy that love filled them with during a particular time in their life. While they live in their illusion, they surrender completely and need nothing else. There are no thoughts or questions. They become totally loved.

This moment in infinity is lovely for them and it is the way they begin to UN-grow. They learn to let go of the things that drove them in life. It is a way to leave all other experiences behind in the wave of a hand.

Pure love is God's way of working their hands.

Chapter Seven

More Ways Wings Lighten Up

In leaving the world, you leave the unnatural world behind and return refreshed to your true place in order to work love to its best ability. That is called Lightening Up. There is the arrival, the illusion, and the process of Lightening Up.

There are other ways to Lighten Up, however, in addition to those we discussed. The one we described earlier applies to new souls arriving here and how they begin to refresh themselves in light, becoming whole again so that they may love purely and totally without the heaviness of life in the world touching them.

For us older souls that have been here longer, Lightening Up is quite a different thing. As white souls that move amongst different layers of love, we love up or we love down, as the need might be. Because we are light, we can use our light to become either more or less dense. This allows us to connect with new souls, as well as old souls. As white beings, we counsel new souls arriving here, in order to help them understand their purpose and their reasons to live within love. Souls are our work and just as you go to work in your daily jobs on earth, we are called to work with those souls needing white love in this place. They are with God, as are we, so there are no strangers here. We all become one once we Lighten Up, whether old souls or new. Once we attain complete whiteness, we work both individually and together, as well.

There is no longer any personality as you know it on earth, no obvious connection to our worldly lives. In Lightening Up, we shed all our physical links and exist solely in love. We exist only to be used by love to help others. There are no time limits, no floor for us to walk on, none of the material things you know in the world. We live in light alone and we are constantly working love without another thought. It is our joy and we use love to create more joy just by working love. Living here in the light, there is no distance, nor time to obey. Even as we are speaking with you, we are able to wash others here with our light, loving them in a different way than we do with you. The part of us that writes this book is lower than the part of us that loves in light.

The way we move without moving at all is the most difficult for humans to understand because we have no body with which to move ourselves from place to place. Think of it as leaving your body at will, but without having a body to leave. The only way we can explain it is that as we Lighten Up, we move deeper into light and love and that is the way we move. There is no end to just how light we can become. There are Lumes, which are more full of light than us Wings, and there is a more enlightened level than theirs, as well. Yet, while they move in a lighter way than we are able, they are still with us in love and its workings.

While Lumes are at a higher level than us and are no longer in direct contact with humans, we Wings work love for both new souls arriving here, as well as looking over souls still living in the world. Each and every soul has others that care for him. People often imagine us swarming around with feathered wings and white gowns, but this is not the case. Angels are only a man made illusion and do not exist, as such, either here in our world or in the physical world. No one here waves at the world in order to be thought of as a God filled angel from above. Those of us that can make contact with humans do so in order to touch our loved ones with more love. That means we must assume the personality we once were in life. Otherwise, we could not comfort them.

Chapter Eight

Ways Wings Connect With Humans

Before we continue, it is important to tell you that we white Wings have wooly halos. Around our heads, above us, is the white light that we have become. It appears like a halo, a nimbus (cloud/vapor) of light, and usually that is how people imagine us. Nouns (humans with names) have auras that cover their outline with pulsing energy. Because we have no bodies, we are totally light. White light. This light is love and it is what we have become. Yes, light is all that we are. We can use our lightness as a way to descend to comfort people in the world or rise to places of pure love.

Things are not always as they seem in the world. People don't usually stop to question the white light that they unconsciously know exists, although they are not fully aware of it. People call this white light "intuition" or a "feeling", but it is the white light of a higher power that they are using to enlighten themselves. Of course, knowing and doing are two different things. Think of it as having an inherent or built in awareness, but not yet having developed the knowledge to use it. As Wings living in the afterworld, we jog (shake, jolt) awareness in others with the intention of waking them up to our presence, but people seldom do awaken to it.

As mentioned above, we have wooly halos, which is our aura. It is the white light that we have become upon our physical deaths. People also have auras that cover the outline of their bodies with pulsing energy. These auras show themselves to us in various colors. We have no bodies, however, to weigh us down, except for the image of a body. Nor do we carry the heavy emotions that are a part of worldly life. We are totally light. White light. This light is love. The light is us and not the other way around. We can love up or love down, which means we can descend to souls in the world or rise up to places of pure love. As we have said before in this book, there is no sound in this place, but there is a type of love that calls sound to it. When one of our soul group members sends a call to love, we hear it and go to assist them.

Apparitions

How do we take on human form? Mankind has worded much about our existence and the general opinion is that we are too farfetched to be true. Most people don't believe we are real because there are no scientific facts to support our existence.

There is no way to prove we exist. Having lived both in the physical world and now living truly in love here, there are things I can tell you about the ways we are able to connect with people.

There are rugged souls who can give humans a visible sign of their existence by making an appearance on earth. They are tougher than some because they have given up earthly life, but still have the strength required to enter the world. These souls have a body that they can take on at will. They assume their old appearance in order to show themselves to the world. This is not easy because, as part of Lightening Up in the afterlife, we work hard to rid ourselves of our body image. Remember, it is bodies that imprison the soul and limit a soul by its existence. Learning to forget our bodies is part of the illusion we are given when we cross over. In the illusion we are given here, we are never overweight or old and frail. We appear the way we did when we were most full of love in our souls.

To return to earth in order to make a "public appearance" is an art that few can use. These special few are able to "put on" the image that others carry of them. An example of this would be seeing a child you remember from a particular time of their life, perhaps as a toddler tugging on your leg or playing on a swing. Pouring oil (love) is how we give to a soul. In pouring oil, we lock into love with the person. So that's another way a Wing connects with humans.

The way a Wing is called to show himself in the world is this... by watching a person's grief or despair he is pulled down by the weight of it. The farther you pull him to you, the more he is to able re-create himself to benefit you. The human becomes awakened by the appearance and the visiting soul is lifted up to the light again. The strength of the mortal's mental image of us is important in making this happen. That's why some people are prone to seeing ghosts, while others never see them. The appearance of the soul is an "electrical illusion". The energy given by the mortal can be used by the soul to step into the person's aura. Love is the energy that is used to do this. The act of appearing is a talent that only some souls possess. This is another reason why we are so seldom seen.

Hovering

When we hover, we use the wave's (mortal that calls out for help) flood of emotions to anchor us down. The force of the person's aura is the way we are able to juggle (align) our vision with theirs. Humans tend to think in images. For us, those images are used to assist us to focus on the whole issue. Damaged love is usually the reason we are called to hover over someone, but in this whole image we can see if the person's pain or wound is calling out to love or willing it away. Willing love away is what a vicious action does. A murderer, for example, disregards love in all its forms by killing another. He ignores his own love and the love of the person he kills. He disregards the victim's families (including his own family) and their wellbeing, as well as the wellbeing of the community. So there is no direction that love can take in that act of willfulness that allows us to connect with that type of soul.

As Wings, we can love the mourners. But, without the images the mourner generates within himself, we could not hover over them. The images leave people like a swirl of color. These colors extend upwards and cover the person who holds them. People are aware of these emotions, too. You see the sad face, but also are aware of joining essences with them, meaning there is still a flow of energy from one person to another that can be felt. When people say, "my heart aches" or "my heart felt heavy" this describes the grief that shows itself in the aura. The color is shown as orange or black. The deeper the color, the heavier you feel.

In joining with a person's aura, we are able to see how wounds affect the person and, again, it allows us to see things from the person's point of view. This, in turn, causes us to view older issues of the person, as well as the current issue, because we are then able to see how the person's thoughts, images and wounds came to be. Hovering in this way makes us wise about what happens next and to whom it will happen. It allows us to see the person's future.

You have many connections in the world, but love is the strongest one. Therefore, you will show aural colors in the same way when someone you love is "off color". Hovering allows us to be drawn into the soul of a person, which then allows us to give them what is needed by using our love.

Pouring Oil

We wish to talk about pouring oil. While we hover above a person, we use oil to soothe the souls we overlook. Pouring oil is just a phrase, but it is a descriptive one, as it implies that we are soothing peoples' souls, oiling them with love, and that is so. While the love we pour may not be immediately felt, it is felt afterwards, which causes a person's life to become less difficult. Once the person's emotions soothe down, the person is less tortured by his own gravity. Having overlooked many, I have seen how this wobbles (jolts into place) a soul, making them more able to be themselves and less distracted or withdrawn. The reasons why we pour oil are simple. We are love and we give love. We cannot withhold it and we overlook others because we love others and because we are made only of the light of love. It is a complete circle that repeats endlessly.

You might imagine that there could come a time when there will be no one left on earth to love. That will never happen and life will always be. Love could not develop worlds at all if it allowed them to be destroyed. As Wings, the nature of mankind is ours to shape and we do this all the time by our presence on earth and by pouring oil. We also have the ability to pull wires. It is our job description to pull them for the good of a person and for the good of love. Love means looking after lives. Hovering allows us to see far beyond that which is visible to you and allows us to make little touches that can have a large effect.

Dreams

The dream state is halfway between two worlds. It can be the place of refreshment for living souls. People go there in their sleep and often drift out of the body. It is a world of glowing, beautiful things.

One way that we can descend to be with people on earth is through their dreams. The dreaming place is halfway between two worlds. It is the place where humans go to refresh their souls. It is a world of glowing things and is a place where thoughts can take shape and join with others' wires, which then makes them happen in peoples' waking lives. Wishing in your dreams for love to come to you, for example, allows your wires, which are the connections of love we share with others, to join two souls. It is a way to connect with your soul mate, even if you have not yet met him or her.

We can often interrupt a dream and that is the usual way most Wings communicate with people. The deceased soul is pulled there by the wave (mortal) that grieves for them or cares enough about the soul to think about him/her. In the dreaming place, we can tap into the mortal's desire to connect with their loved one because the dreamer is passive and can be touched by us.

In the dreaming place, people hang like birds caught in a net. Dreams are the wonderful ways the mind sorts out all that goes on in one's life. The dreaming place is light... like twilight. Because Wings have the ability to move through time and God's world, we can join mortals there. We touch them with love through our presence. There are many people who don't remember their dreams, but awaken the next morning with a new feeling of peace or cheer because of our presence.

What about evil spirits that appear in dreams?

That's a lot of hooey. Remember that there are no evil souls wandering about in our world. All become as one in the light of love. No man, despite convincing himself that evil exists or believes himself to be evil, has ever looked into the face of love and been able to withstand the overwhelming power of love. These "evil" fantasies are manmade stories and are the childhood stories of wooden (dull, lifeless) men who know nothing about the true meaning of light and its souls.

In the dreaming place, lives warm themselves and fend for themselves, as well. It is not always a glimpse of heaven. It is much more complex.

The way Wings tag a person with in dreams is like

this....

There is much that is ugly in the dreaming place. The bad dreams you have usually take place in the mind, but not up here. Because the mind is where man's images are created, there are right and wrong ones. Dreams are very much like a junk shop full of odds and ends. A person can find another's image while dreaming, find that it fits him, and adopt it as his own. There are no ownership rights there. Having adopted an image, it can take precedent over a person's previous images in dreams. In other words, Wings can touch the person with images in dreams that are designed to enlighten him. He may wonder later where this "new thought" came from later, but by bonding with it in his dream, it becomes tied to him.

In the dreaming place you are free of external images and are able to really look around. Many beautiful images of the afterlife are available to see while people dream. Those that have seen these places through the mind's eye never forget these images. There is a clarity and a heart stopping beauty to that which the dreamer sees while he is sleeping. It is in these moments of true sleep that one's soul ventures forth into this place of beauty and glory. It is the place where mortal man can witness far more than in his daily, worldly life.

Some people dream of crystal waters, which is the soul-soothing place, where the water seems to be alive. The colors of the water are translucent, yet very vivid, and they are like balm to the viewer, soothing tired souls. They are given a light that fills them, rather than a light that only allows vision. In this place, there is a sound of soft enormity that fuels, rather than depletes one's soul.

There are also visions of future events for some, which sometimes warn them of impending events that have yet to take place. These are usually given to the sleeper through the wires that connect Wings with their loved ones, in order to show the person what lies in store for them.

Most people experience a union between souls easily when they have lost a loved one through death. It is unfortunate that people mourn, of course, but it is also a natural reaction when we must accept the fact that the person we thought we possessed in life is not actually ours to keep, but are just here on loan. When a mortal reaches out in love, it allows us to join with them in the dreaming place or by filling ourselves with that person's energy and descending to earth.

Other ways we can make our presence known or felt to people is like this... writing... and we can talk directly to some people.

That is the limit of our abilities, really. When people have near death experiences (man's definition, not ours) they often speak of seeing a tunnel of light. Or seeing loved ones again and, for some, the sense of regret felt upon returning to the physical world. These are real descriptions of encounters with love and we feel happy knowing that we are recognized by many as living in a beautiful place that is just out of reach.

Chapter Nine

Ricky

If we're fortunate, we make a few true friendships in the course of a lifetime. If we're truly blessed, we meet one person that remains our best friend through thick and thin, no matter how close or far apart. Ricky was mine. In Chapter Five, I mentioned a visit that Ricky paid me one night when I was feeling a little down in the dumps. His appearance removed any lingering doubts about the existence of life after death that might have remained. Of the many problems I've *faced in nearly sixty years of living, hallucinations has not been one of them. There is no question his appearance was real and I know that he visited to comfort an old friend who was having a bad day. Imagine my surprise years later, when a spiritual medium asked if I knew someone named Ricky and informed me that he was one of the Seven Writers of this book.*

Ricky's death was a difficult one. He was a young man in his mid-twenties when he fell from the back of a moving truck after one beer too many. He cracked his skull on the pavement and fell into a coma. The prognosis was irreversible brain damage and Ricky was hooked to a life-support machine, where he would remain for the next twelve years. It was later explained to me that he hovered above his lifeless body in a state of limbo for the entire time, along with a spirit guide. His soul could not leave his hospital room until his body completely shut down, however, and his body couldn't shut down as long as it was connected to a ventilator.

On the other hand, the extra time allowed Ricky's spirit guide to give him a preview of the Lightening Up process, while waiting for his body to die. As a result, he was able to move through the viewing and illusion process faster than most new souls arriving in the afterlife. The other Six Writers of the soul group say that he has become more of a free spirit than most. Ricky always was a bit on the carefree and irreverent side during earthly life and remains much the same in the next world, as you will see in his words.

There is a white Wing here with a lively way about him and he waits to write his chapter for the book. We think he will be a lovely addition, just wait until you hear him!

This wave says call me Buddy, as in Buddy Holly. I was a young boy while he sang on the radio and I really love those old singers.

Have you ever had a good accident? There is nothing like

a really good accident to wake you up. It makes you aware that life is not just something to be taken for granted, but is also a blessing. Small matters fade out altogether when we are given a reality jolt, but I open the talk this way in order to introduce the experience of dying.

Dying is the most mysterious marvel that man locks horns with in his physical life. Everyone knows they will die one day and nobody wants to think too much about it. Enormous amounts of money are spent looking after health and continued existence, but very little money is required to die. Dying is cheap, but staying alive is damned expensive. There are funeral expenses to be paid, of course, but that comes after the death itself. Embalming a body is just a placebo, a sugar coating designed to postpone the mourners' fears of being buried in the ground. Oddly enough, though, mourners in the old days would begin to heal after viewing a loved one's body in the front room of a house for a few days. It gave people time to see the changes that death makes to a body. In doing so, people can see that the dead person is no longer the loved one they knew in life. After a day or two, the unpreserved body ceases to even resemble the person they knew for so many years. This is normal and it's a grave subject. This is digging deep, for sure. I want this to be written with humor because it is a serious subject. Dead serious, and it should be Lightened Up with humor.

In his effort to conquer his environment and postpone the inevitable, modern man tries to perpetuate physical life. He attempts to cheat death, using vitamins and pills and modern medicine and machinery. Humans strive so hard, both as people and societies, to keep themselves alive and when someone close does die, it comes as a complete and utter blow to the core of one's awareness as a human. Why does man fear death so much? It is because so much effort is put into mortal living that death goes against the grain of all we are taught in life. Things like childbirth, raising and nurturing a child are ways people create bonds, naturally, and people fear that they will never see their loved ones again after death, though we do see them again.

Accepting a loved one's death is far less difficult for those with faith that life after death exists, however. It's those without faith that most fear death.

So people dress their loved ones up, even in death. They see them laid out in a casket all flashed up, dressed to kill. What they don't see is the folding tent the human body becomes after its heart stops beating. This dressing up of the body detracts from the reality that death is a part of life and denies that the personality of their loved one is also dead. People don't get the opportunity to take proper leave of their loved ones these days.

People love one another's egos, their little physical traits and mannerisms. The sound of a voice, their laugh, or the way the person walks. These things create the mental images we love about a person. But take away the body upon death, we also take away the brain and ego part of the person we knew and loved. What is it that people really mourn when that happens?

They mourn for themselves. They grieve thinking that they will never see or interact with that person again. It is the physical package combined with the ego that creates worldly love and it is that loss which mourners wail over when a loved one dies. It's a normal reaction, after all, because that is the way people live together.

If you see a corpse in all its disintegrating glory, however, the experience de-personalizes the loved one. The mourner then wakes up to the fact that the physical changes that follow death have changed this loved one of theirs beyond recognition. The reason I am writing this for Danny is to show you, the reader, that the only thing that has actually gone is the body. Our souls, our unseen light and inner spark, fly upwards to rejoin the light as easily as a drop of mercury flows back to itself. We literally Lighten Up upon our physical death, but the essence of us, our soul, remains intact and lives on eternally.

Now I'll explain the process of death and what happens

after we get there. When a body dies, the shutting down of the system takes only a moment. I'm talking about the actual moment of death here, which doesn't happen the minute we stop breathing. Although the heart stops in the dying process, there is still the winding down of the body that must be completed before a soul can completely leave the body. Blood still moves slowly through the veins and there is still oxygen remaining in the lungs. Bit by bit, the body dies completely, and this takes a long time. Although there are many variables, the complete and total death of a body generally requires about four hours time.

During this winding down of the body, the living memories of one's soul and mind are still intact and the aura that surrounds the body is still visible. It is during this time that a soul sees the review of his or her life. They can see their loved ones cry, watch as their toe is tagged, or even witness the type of treatment their body receives at the morgue. They are able to see just what they actually were like as people and exactly how they affected others during their life. It is overwhelming for the new soul to witness. A rouged, oval aura surrounds the new soul while reviewing his or her life. It is a pale shade of pink, which lights the soul. This color represents the half and half state of the soul during this new beginning and the new soul then joins what he once thought were his deceased loved ones upon death. The death is expected by those souls that watch over a person during their life on earth and so they have a "welcome wagon" of souls awaiting them, so to speak. These are his soul group members.

The new soul is warmly welcomed and well assisted in waking up to this place of light and love. By the time the viewing is over, the body has expired completely and the soul loves the illusion he is being given in order to help him in his new life as a soul. Which just happens to be the gift of living in pure and total love. This gift is much more than his ego-driven wants and needs ever knew in his worldly life. He is literally drawn to the light by the overwhelming feeling of love that pulls and draws the soul to it.

In most cases, the soul answers to the call of love. Whether young or old, lit or unlit soul, he is given the illusion in order to heal the wounds that all souls suffer in their mortal lives. But, for some, especially those that died tragically or suddenly, the loved ones he left behind often grieve deeply. Their heavy emotions hold the soul in its grip, like a trap. This is a very difficult place for a soul to be stuck, as he is being pulled down at the same time he is trying to rise, to Lighten Up. The events of the death itself have no affect on the soul, no matter how horrific the death had been. Once the soul leaves its body it has no concerns with the memories of dying. Who really remembers the shock of being born, after all? It is simply a passage, a transition, and is unimportant. The soul is now at home in love as it never was on earth.

Although we tell you that the mourners hold the soul back when they cry for their loved one, grief is a normal thing and should be expressed. But prolonged or excessive grief or the hatred many mourners feel in the case of murder, for example, holds the soul in its rosy red aura until the power of their grief abates. We wish that we could comfort the living mourners in these horrible cases, but the sheer heaviness of their grief makes it very difficult to touch many of them with our love. The mourner needs love, especially at this time, yet it is hard for us to comfort them when they wrap themselves in sorrow. We work constantly and tirelessly in the wisest ways, always, and we work to assist the new soul arriving here, as well as the living. We are neither patient nor impatient when working with others. Our entire purpose is to give love. Love Is Us, Incorporated.

Have you ever walked through a cemetery? Place your faith and joy in the walk itself. Don't focus on the graves you see there. Enjoy the day and the life you've been given. Focus on loving and living, as these are the reasons you were given the gift of life. Keep your faith strong in the knowledge that there is life after death for us all. Celebrate the happiness and joy that you and your deceased loved one spent together, rather than weighing them and yourself down with sadness. Life has no choice but to continue when the body dies, because the soul is the spark of light and love, which survives and thrives in all things. There is no brain to produce emotion once the body dies and there is no need to feel pain. Describe color to a blind man. It is what we are doing with these words when we try to describe living in this place. We are trying to give to all who read this book the immensity of the light and love that we become as souls after physical death. We have none of the human emotions after death. The way that we love others is a beneficial thing, certainly, yet we are not feeling love. We are love.

Whatever you do in life, and however you do it, remember this. Your purpose is to appreciate living on earth as the way to express the finest, most joyful part of yourself! Use the magic of the personality you possess for your own care. In doing so, you will create the same, both for others and in others.

Love in the world is a confusing thing. It is usually at the mercy of things such as the mind and body's health, its thoughts and its fears. But the love that is the light of creation is beyond all these meddling things. Look around you. See the trees, the sky, even the cars we drive and houses around us. All are built from someone's love. Love is quiet, yet it shouts out its existence everywhere you look! Everything is created through love and so are you. You are a marvel, a perfect gift to the world. That is the meaning of a human being.

Share the realizations of this book with others. Have faith, always, that life is larger than yourself and will always lead you back to your beginning.

Part Two

How The Wings Want You To Live. And Don't.

Chapter Ten

How Not To Live

Today we will talk about the man made issues that souls now battle in the world. There was never a time when living was easy, no matter who you were in life. Life is about struggle, as well as joy. People are often forced to deal with ungodly sins like war and the oppression of freedom just to live out their natural lives. In today's world, man ignores his need to give worship to his God. This new ignorance of worship is mostly because many people don't feel the need to appease God anymore. Man can get all he wants by using society. He can supply his own needs without bowing to anyone or anything. Our point is that, while man governs himself with material desires, his spiritual side goes ignored. He stands alone, without any reason to consider that spiritual love is important. Managing himself isn't what he is meant to do, but for a while things go his way and life seems very good. Who needs God, anyway? This is the way many people think in today's world. Who needs healing from above when hospitals perform miracles without divine intervention? Who needs to worry about life immortal when the here and now is more important? So, many a man goes about his life without giving a second thought to old beliefs.

These days, people worship little green spacemen, sports heroes and pop stars. There is no one more given to using words than mankind and he has always given words to that which he "feels" to be true, as well as those things he wants to believe. While his beliefs might not always be accurate, his intuition is usually on target. Man is aware that we do exist in his unconscious mind and it shows in his speech when he says things like "God help me" or "Oh, my God". Everyone, atheists and believers alike, calls upon us at some point in their lives.

Many humans have no interest in looking upwards towards God. All they feel they need are the material things they haven't got and they devote themselves only to getting that which they think they need. It is simply a way to pass time, but it is not the only way. Most people spend their time walking blindly through their lives, obsessing about unimportant things and driven by the need to acquire more unimportant things. These people rarely stop to think about more than just the human need to hunt and possess. Though we must do this in the world, to an extent, we mustn't forget that worldly life is not the beginning of life, nor the end. That is how humanity survives at its lowest level, but having a soul gives mankind the ability to reach beyond those basic instincts.

People have become more like hermits in their lives. Computers, television, phone calls to the other side of the world have become the way people interact these days. Front porches have become backyard decks so people don't have to see their neighbors. As we have repeated throughout this book, love is an energy that defines life. How can love be expressed and shared with others if people live insulated lives and stay holed up in their homes like hermits? Even within the home, family members isolate themselves from one another. The love that is life is made to flow. How can it do so when people lock themselves away inside their homes because of their fear of one another and the world outside their front door?

Modern man leaves no stone unturned in his desire to rule and possess everything. It makes him feel powerful to be self-rewarding. The time has arrived to remind people that mortal life is not the main act, but is just the dress rehearsal for the real show. Man needs to understand that his actions in the physical world shape his soul. His soul, in turn, shapes the souls of others. If we Wings can cause a few people to view life with new eyes, then we love with the right intentions. With this as our new focus, we are willing to build this understanding with you. We can't live for you, however, and you must also focus and give yourself to applying the words we offer you. There is time enough to do everything in your day, but make the teachings of this book your main focus.

When I went to the grave I took final memories with me. They are happy memories of a family that was alive in the world and embracing and giving to life. People shared a love that was ever growing, always expanding, as they lived lives without fear of the people around them. Looking at people today, I see how a lack of faith affects not only their lives, but also those that surround them. Some souls arriving here upon their deaths have often spent their entire lives in fear. Many have lived their whole lifetime without faith and that, in turn, inhibited all they did in their lives. A lack of faith shut down the connection between them and those they were close with in life. In doing so, they blocked the flow of love, which caused ups and downs in the lives of all involved.

There will always be times in your life when one's faith is shaken, when circumstances seem unjust or overwhelming. But, if we let those moments and the doubts, fear and utter dread of living overtake us, then life becomes full of blockages and obstacles, both in our social/public lives and in our private lives, as well.

Take excessive drinking, for example, which is often a result of living a fearful and faithless life. If you drink too much, the effects eventually become obvious to everyone. Bills don't get paid, work life suffers, and the drinker's loved ones are neglected and abused. Even if there is no physical or verbal abuse, the love between the drinker and his family is abused. Over time, the bottle takes full control and everything the alcoholic does revolves around drinking. It is obvious to everyone.

Yet, people who don't drink to excess, but live without faith, don't see that they also affect their loved ones in the same way. Their behavior is every bit as harmful as the alcoholic's, just less obvious. As is the situation with the heavy drinker, most people refuse to acknowledge that there's a problem at all. It's not me, they say. It's the state of the world today. The blame lies with the terrorists or others living in the world. They cannot understand that by limiting themselves in so many small ways, they stop the flow of love dead in its tracks. That is when vague, undefined little acts of loveless, hostile behavior begin happening. Pent up anger, for example, is a natural reaction when love is denied to a person.

The fact that money has become so plentiful, yet so unevenly shared, has become another problem that holds men hostage in the world. Half the world has too much and half, or more, has little or nothing in the way of food, shelter, money and possessions. The desire for money is part of the "hunt and kill" motivation that drives man. If money brought people happiness, we would be out of jobs here in the afterlife. There would be no need to reassure souls of anything but more money. There is no tally taken to tell us when we have enough, so people go on amassing more "stuff". They use their energy to be always looking for something new to add to their possessions, be it furniture they don't need or more food than is healthy. This causes men to live blindly, in a vacuum, with their eyes focused on the next thing to "get" instead of looking at the whole picture. To live simply, without all the toys, is harder because it takes away all the manufactured thoughts that fill a void within these people.

"I support myself" is a popular slogan in today's day and age, which equates generating one's own income with having full power over one's destiny. Although there is nothing wrong with being self-employed, people too often confuse self-reliance with happiness. Money does not buy happiness and people mustn't confuse the freedom of choice that comes with money with inner peace and happiness. Man needs to appreciate things he already possesses within himself, such as his personality, his spiritual side, and the freedom to live in a state of love. These are the true gifts he's been given and these gifts should be backed by an awareness of his reason for being. Which is to rise above life's obstacles and to learn to Lighten Up. Man needs to understand that living in an awareness of love is his true purpose in life.

A life lived to suit yourself is a selfish thing and is unfulfilling. While we hope people will benefit from this book, we really want to help people restore their faith in life. There is a difference between hope and faith. Hope comes from giving with the anticipation of being rewarded. Faith is more than hope. Faith is knowing that rewards come from giving, but the rewards received are of another kind. The reason it is important to have faith is because faith is investment. It is an investment into your own future, both in this life and the next. Having faith gives you the realization that there is more to life than having everything and everyone you want. It creates a justice, of sorts. If a man lives in the awareness that his acts should be pleasing to his God, then he is willingly waging a war against the darker, more selfish people who act without fear of judgment.

It is not our desire to change mankind or to belittle him. We talk only so that people might listen and learn to live happily. We join in this book in order to assure man that the love he felt at the finest moment of his earthly life is just a small fraction of the joy he will feel when his soul leaves his body and reunites with the one living thing that exists wholly and eternally... love. We don't expect people to become martyrs or saints.

People are no better off sacrificing themselves than anyone else in order to win "merit points" in their mortal lives. There is no judgment given in the next life where one soul is better than another, after all. We don't ask anyone to take a vow of poverty or sacrifice their own happiness to help others. To sacrifice anything basically means to kill it and the same applies to the lives people live. How can a soul live a happy, fulfilled life if it must subdue itself in order to live? We simply want you to share the love within your soul with others. Love is where you were created and love is where you will return when your body ceases to live.

In any case, we don't give "extra points" to those who are love filled and give of themselves to the poor, although it may very well be someone's natural tendency to do these things. In that case, they are expressing themselves as they should, which is a good thing. It is only when people live without expressing themselves in a loving way that they are living wrongly. Living without expressing oneself naturally affects everyone else in one way or another. Expressing oneself as we were designed to live also benefits everyone we meet, which is, of course, living a life of faith and love.

Chapter Eleven

Man's Morals and Human Issues

In the last chapter, some of the souls' words about us mere mortals might seem a little harsh, at times, or even condescending. But that is not the case. There is no judgment from them and there is a lot of truth to the problems they address, as well. This chapter discusses earthly issues, as viewed by the Wings from their world. Because these issues have an effect on how we live in this world, I decided to include them with the "How To Live" section of this book, rather than include them in Part One, which describes life in the Wings' world.

Morals

There is much wickedness in the lives of some people. It is greater than ever before because there is too much plenty (excess) in the world today. Crimes are committed because people want more. They want more sex, more money, and more power. They discover that by ignoring love for their fellow man, they are free to fulfill their basic instincts and satisfy their own selfish needs. By denying love, a man can deny that he is dealing with other people on a human level. He overlooks their need for love and thinks only of his own wants and needs. It becomes easy to kill others if you give them no good attributes. It's easy to take a human life if you don't appreciate life yourself and it's easy to cheat and steal to acquire things, rather than look for the true value of earning them through self-discipline and hard work. It becomes easier to cheat both others and yourself than it is to sacrifice the smaller comforts of life in order to receive the truly valuable gifts of living.

Love, however, has no morals. Love is simply love and, as such, cannot hold a grudge or find exception with its perfect self. There are souls in the afterlife that are filled with light and those that are lightless, but love makes no distinction between them. Those that have light within their souls are not snobs. They view all men on earth in the same way that we do in this place of love and light. All need love and all are given love, whether they are Wings or Unlit Souls.

Those that ignore the rules of society are judged by society. Both man's legal system and society have laws for every situation. These are man's laws and are written by man, not by us. On earth, the only way that civilization and societies could thrive and survive is through these laws, of course. Without them, there would be only chaos and a dog-eat-dog existence. Anger over one bad deed generates more of both, just as living generates more life.

We don't need morals in this place because sin does not exist here. Only love exists and there is no inclination by any soul to "take advantage of the system". Once removed from our bodies, we look upon the world with love and we see the smallness of gouging (hurting) others. We view the pettiness of human wants (ego-driven behavior), be it for money, lust, or the insatiable need for power that those who are devoid of love use to hurt and oppress others.

The so-called sins of people, when viewed from a distance, are pitiful things and are not at all shocking to us. From our vantage point, there is only love to be allotted to those below. I use the word allotted because each soul has an issue – a wound - that he or she is given in his lifetime on earth. Some arrive to us with very little love because their souls are unlit. They are unenlightened and without the light of love to guide them in their worldly lives. While they live in the physical world, they have only human love to help them along. We help turn the wheels of life for those people while they walk the earth, in order to assist them in the world.

You might see these as acts of luck, but it isn't blind luck at all. Nor is it favoritism. It is just easier for us to arrange the good fortune of people when there is very little involved in a life. Wings on earth usually have complex issues to deal with and they choose worldly life in order to work those issues out. The earthbound Wing doesn't need luck. He needs love, plain and simple. A Wing's life often appears harder than many, but how else can one's soul rise unless there is a reason for it to rise? Those in need of love are given it. Those in need of a chance to improve in other ways, which is the case with unlit souls, are often given "lucky" opportunities to assist them in life. Every person has the ability to change his or her circumstances in life, yet some do not, regardless of the opportunities they are given.

The Wing that applies faith and love in life floats to the top, rather than sinking to the bottom. He or she rises above difficult challenges in life.

Heaven and Hell and Karma

Animals... cats, dogs, and even insects have auras and return to the light upon physical death. There is no life created by love that does not return here. There is no evil anywhere, except in the actions of one man to another. We Wings call these vicious acts Godless and there are no Godless souls here. There are soulless people on earth, and that is where they stay, but all souls return to this place.

The truth is that there is no day of reckoning here for any soul. Those people who want judgment passed on others for the

Godless acts they've committed in their human lifetimes only wound themselves with their judgments. These people need to learn faith and acceptance. We know many people think it is forgiveness that must be given, not faith and acceptance. That is not the truth. Charity within one's heart is another thing that many people believe in, as well, but that is also not really the case. To forgive certainly sets you apart from others, but it can also make one feel smug and superior and that is wrong. Again, all souls are equal in this place of love and light. It is only the actions of mortal man that creates inequity. Those that sin are not inferior to any other in the eyes of love. Man's earthly view is that a person is lesser to another if he has no education or money, but he is lesser only in worldly matters.

The "sinner" is someone that has become overwhelmed by life, for one reason or another. He or she has become detached from love and from spirit, usually due to the wounds inflicted on them by others. We know that the soul of a killer is never alone, but his mind has created feelings of loneliness and separateness within him. He is blind to our presence, but we are aware of him. It is his inability to make the correct emotional or mental connections that cause his actions. This is the reason he cannot control himself or behave in the way society requires of him. His behavior is unacceptable only in society's eyes, not in love's eyes. If he creates damage to others' lives, however, he should be separated from society. If he doesn't learn to Lighten Up on earth, his soul will eventually be returned to the light to be healed.

This is another reason to emphasize that there is no devil or Prince of Darkness... none. There are no dark forces within the universe directing man. Any evil act that man commits results directly from his physical life. It is usually a combination of his chemical and emotional make up. A baby is created through a physical process and takes blind luck as to what it becomes. A soul is trapped within that body, usually, and it is the light contained in the soul that gives man his finest abilities as a human. The soul may be introduced to the world along with the human's wounds, whether they are environmental or physical in their nature. But a Wing never comes into the world to cause destruction. He or she comes only to spread light and love.

The challenge for every person is to spread light and love in the world and not to block them. There is no karmic wheel whereby a human is created with the intention to pay someone or something back in life or to be paid back for the actions of a previous lifetime. All come to live in the best way they are able, plain and simple, and all have the ability to make choices to do just that every day.

Romantic Love

Falling in love is like ointment to the ego and it is only that. All couples that live together for a long time are far removed from being that exhilarated couple that first came together. The love between a husband and wife is only successful when both parties choose for it to be successful. A love is not broken or given to another elsewhere unless one or both people in a relationship have made that choice. If one decides to withhold love from the other by focusing on another person, or just due to the many problems and issues that are bound to invade any couple's life, they block the flow of love between them. The ego is what is actually hurt in any heartbreak. It is not a wound of either the soul or the body, although the body may suffer as the result of a wounded ego. The ego-driven images of love that people hold in human life do not change. Romantic love is a part of mortal life and that is where "love vs. love" becomes involved.

A long relationship based upon mutual giving and commitment to the better of both people does not suffer from changes that occur in a relationship over time. Instead, the couple adapts to these changes, providing that the love that flows between them is based upon faith. If one person loses faith in the other, though, things begin to fall apart. Once love is blocked by one or both parties' refusal to commit totally to one another, romantic love begins to flounder and causes those involved to feel devastated by their loss.

Keeping faith an active part of a couple's love does two things. Faith in a higher love enriches a couple's life together and also causes one's ego to be ever-willing to extend itself to love, whether it be through swallowing one's pride or admitting our fears to the one we love. When two people love one another in this way there is no need to harbor pain and resentments towards one another, even if the relationship does eventually fail. Acceptance of a failed relationship is easy if you have faith in life. Faith allows you to move on in the knowledge that having love within yourself is a far better way to live than any romp in the hay.

The saying, "It is better to have loved and lost than never to have loved" is very true. Whether we become separated from our partner because of death or through a failed relationship, you become richer by learning to understand acceptance, once the grieving passes. You become richer in your acceptance and brighter in your faith. In other words, that which doesn't kill us makes us stronger. Not because you survived a failed relationship or marriage, but because you learned it was better to allow your love to express itself to the best of your ability, even if one or both of you could not do so during your time together.

There is no failure in love. If worldly love fails you, that's no reason to shut the door to your heart and block the flow of love - either to you or from you. All that will do is to create a wound for you or others that will continue to grow worse as time goes on. Choose to always keep the faith. If things don't work out between you and the other person, use your faith to accept it and move on with your life. Choose to apply love in all you do in life and life will always reward you with more love. It will always flow both to you and from you.

Reincarnation, Karma and Conception

How Wings Return To Mortal Life – Birth Of A Wing

There is no judgment given here and no karmic wheel or law that applies when a soul returns to earth in the body of a newborn child. A murderer in a past life is not sent back to become a murder victim in the next life, nor must a wealthy man return to experience poverty. As Wings, we return to earth in order to further Lighten Up as souls by spreading love and by using love to rise above any obstacles we encounter in life.

The way we are called to earth is by a call from a

member of our soul group, as we have also mentioned earlier. We descend in order to become earthbound Wings and the way we are conceived into life works in the following way.

The gift of life is a wonderful thing. It creates joy within a pregnant woman, even while it may dismay her to be pregnant. The way that life just goes about its business without concern for the circumstances of the parents is almost humorous. Life will fulfill itself regardless of man's attempts to obstruct it. There is always a chance in every conception that we Wings will be conceived into a pregnancy that will be terminated. It matters little to us, however, as the soul will be returned here to the light in the event of a failed pregnancy and the process will repeat again - if not with the same mother, then with another member of our soul group.

The child's mother usually makes the call that brings us down, but it can be a call from any member of the family who is closely attached to the mother, such as an aunt or grandfather, for example. The call is not so much a request as it is a bequest, because it is something people inherit by being part of the soul group. It is quite literally the gift of life.

Wings enjoy living physical lives. It is a way for us to best express the job we do, with all life's ups and downs included. Although death means little to us Wings because all souls return to the afterlife upon their deaths, physical life is never meaningless. Without exception, a Wing comes to earth to answer a call of love, as a God given gift of love to both his soul group and to the world. There are many things involved in this process. Firstly, we receive the call and we descend to be with the mother. We might have a short wait or a long one while waiting for the conception to occur, but time is unimportant to us. We use the time while we wait to work our love on an earthly level. We wait until the moment of conception has arrived and once the woman's seed is fertilized, all systems are go. We give ourselves to the woman's body and are absorbed both into her body and her soul. The process is similar to melting and we melt into the mother. In doing so, we become a part of her, which is why a mother's bond of love with her child is like no other. The soul of the child has its roots in the mother's soul, in her light.

The entry is a slow one. There is no jolt felt when she subconsciously becomes aware of the addition, but she is aware of a feeling of joy within her. While this is a "time out" for us, cooperation from the embryo is required as to whether or not it is forming properly. We have no control over this once we become part of the child's body. It is a gamble based upon our faith in love and there is many a slip betwixt cup and lip, as the saying goes.

So, we are now within our new mother and as the seed of love begins to grow, we fill it. The mother, after all, has a soul of her own and doesn't need us. The child does need us, though, in order to become a lit soul in life. We fill the baby's soul in small increments at first, until gradually the unborn child is filled with our love. Upon conception, we lose all awareness of our mission as Wings and we abide within the child without thought or question. This is how Wings return to earthly lives.

Birth of an Unlit Soul

Women with unlit souls can call to love, too, but they normally don't and their children are usually born with unlit souls, as well. This is because water seeks its own level. A Wing, however, cannot ever smother itself by being born into an unlit soul. There would not be enough room for us to spread our light there and we would not be able to acclimate ourselves into life. The societies with the highest death rates on earth have many unlit souls within their populations. There is no disadvantage to that when they later arrive here. As we have said throughout this book, all souls are treated with equal love. All we are is love, and love is all that we do here. But a body containing an unlit soul also means that light doesn't try to fill conditions that do not support it.

What slows the growing tide of unlit souls? They slow it themselves, by their very nature. Most die sooner than others because of their environments, often through war or famine or disease. Their governments are not guided by love or wisdom, so life is not nurtured or protected. Life left to look after itself goes on, but not as successfully without the enlightened souls within a society that create the flow of love and, hence, create the better things in life. The unlit souls arriving here often do return to life on earth, but tend to go round and round in circles of birth and death without refining themselves upon their return to the light. They usually return to earth without Lightening Up. It's important to remember that every soul can Lighten Up if he allows love to fill his or her soul. They must be willing to work to open themselves to it, however.

The Wing always returns to earth in order to assist others and spread love. In doing so, he or she Lightens Up again and again, more and more, each and every time he or she returns to the afterlife.

Abortion

Abortion is a popular choice these days and naturally, as in all things, we make no judgment about it. We are aware before we are conceived into the mother that she might terminate her pregnancy. But, in faith, we do our part to assist life. For us, we are recycled back to love, regardless of whether or not we are born into the world. No harm is done to us by not being born into a body, but abortion can be harmful to the mother, due to the act of denying love to her child and to herself. Bearing a child is a very basic instinct of human life and cannot be terminated without consequences. The symptoms often suffered after an abortion are physical, in part, due to the mother's body being deprived of fulfilling its basic nature.

There is also the withdrawal of our light from within her, which has a profound effect on the woman. Even though she was not fully aware of our presence within her, she "knew without knowing" that her unborn child had already been filled with the light of love and had been shaping itself into a feeling, living person day by day.

After conception has taken place, most women have already created an internal awareness of the child's sex and have a mental image of a boy or a girl. Some even have names for the child. We give this name to her when we fill the love within her soul. These names are given as links to the child's soul group and they are a part of the unconscious awareness that humans possess within themselves. The name a baby arrives with is just one part of the awareness a mother has without realizing it.

As Wings, we simply return to love in the event of an unborn baby. There are no wounds within us to be healed, no dismay over the failure. We are overflowing with love, always, and we have all of eternity to share our love with others. We might or might not return to the same mother next time, but we will return to life. Whether we return as a human vegetable or a rocket scientist makes little difference to us. We are love and we will be expressed in one form or another, regardless.

Love is never scathed by the death of the unborn, but it does cause a scar on the woman. She will grieve and carry the wound of rejecting life and love. This, in turn, may cause her to commit errors of judgment that only deepen the wound she carries. She could turn to drugs or alcohol, for example. For any mother-to-be, we say to be careful what you do. Take responsibility for your body and the outcome of your decisions, because no one else has the power to do it for you. Nor can they save you from the consequences.

Only you can do that.

Suicide

Suicide is a very different type of subject. All life is precious because it carries and creates love. Even the smallest and most basic of life forms have love watching over them and have love within their life. Life is full of cause and effect. Not only in the choices we make, but also in the way we make them. Life is about our willingness to use faith in order to accept life with all its joys and sorrows. We should all use faith as the key to the love that lies within us as the way to keep love and life flowing to everyone and everything.

The soul that is freed from a body by suicide does not return here tormented or restless. Every soul always returns to love to be healed from life's wounds and to Lighten Up. No one arrives here without some wound he carried in mortal life.

The suicidal person takes more than just his own life through his actions, however. He also takes love away from those he has wounded, which causes much sadness and grief for the loved ones he's left behind. By doing this, he has stopped love in its tracks. Those left behind are forced to battle with the sadness he has caused, as well as the mystery of why he would turn away from their love for him. This mourning is very powerful and will hold the soul of the suicidal person as long as it takes for the grieving process below to cease, in the same way grief holds any soul down.

There is no judgment given here by us, as we always say, but that soul does spend a much longer time in the healing process than most. He is suspended in the healing illusion we give him here, while at the same time being pulled downward by the earthly tears and frustration he has caused for those that love him. He is able to clearly see the damage he has done and it takes quite a long time for the suicidal soul to Lighten Up.

We do not recommend that people use suicide as a way out of human life. Life is a gift, after all, and disregarding this gift harms those that gave him love on earth. There is no sin in suicide. There is, however, a right way and a better way to do things. If a person feels so deprived in life that his only thought is to end it, it shows a complete lack of faith on his part. This will be healed and repaired after his physical death, but he will carry the heavy burden of watching over those he has harmed by his actions. It is a case of the punisher, which is partly the motivation for most suicides, now wearing the shoe on the other foot. It is such an unnecessary lesson for one to learn, don't you think?

Life Support

Modern medicine has discovered ways to keep the dead alive. Everyone needs an artificially living corpse in his or her life! I must say I am glad I died before such nonsense came into being. In his ego-driven cleverness, man pats himself on the back as he defies death. But what has he really accomplished? There is no reason to keep a failed body suspended between life and death. In many cases of coma, and most certainly in the case of artificially operated breathing, the brain has already died.

The person's soul, however, is unable to entirely leave the body until it has completely shut down, and so the soul is forced to hover over his lifeless body until it is disconnected from the machines keeping it alive. He can view his body and the people surrounding his body, etc., but is unable to make the full transition between the world below and the next one. He waits in limbo.

As souls, we have all the time in the world, but the soul left hanging does become frustrated with this state of affairs. It is like being tied down in a desert with a glass of water just out of reach. The only good thing to come out of life support is that the mourning process has usually passed by the time he is finally released from his body and he is, therefore, able to make a quick ascension into the Light on his arrival here.

Once again, there is no sin in it. But holding a loved one back is a selfish act on the part of the living.

Death Penalty

There is no man that cannot give to others just by expressing himself, regardless of how his giving measures up from another's point of view. Take a violent criminal, for example. He may have committed the worst acts possible and still feels no shame or remorse for his actions. He is a man without kindness or conscience. Yet, once removed from those he harms, he can still live out the gift of his own life in other ways. This is why there is no judgment given to any soul upon his arrival here.

All have love given to them here in this place and have love to give, as well. His cruel actions in life are due to a blockage of love within him. This blockage was a result of wounds within him that he was either unable or unwilling to overcome during his life. When the body dies, however, the wounded ego within his personality dies along with it and all souls have no choice but to rejoin the Light. All souls originate from the same source, which is the Light of Love.

That having been said, we cannot say that giving mortal life to all men is a good thing. If a man creates more tears than joy in life, there really is no reason for that person to continue life on earth. He can be dead to the world and be reborn in pure Light again and the love he receives here will mend the wounds he carried in his physical life.

There is much debate over the death sentence and yet, we wonder why that is, really. If you know as you do now that life is eternal and that the lifetime of a person is just a tiny drop in the ocean, where lies the harm in removing that drop? Some people will argue that we learn from others` terrible lives or actions, but that is a false argument. What lesson has man ever learned from its despots and criminals? Take Hitler, for example. Look at the way he ravaged the world with his terror and merciless nature and how his drop in the ocean caused huge ripples that continue to this day. He seduced so many people and murdered so many more for no other reason than to satisfy his own ego.

Man has learned nothing from this episode in history. Mass murder, war and genocide still continue today and they will continue in the future. Some people still follow Hitler's doctrines of lunacy and hatred to this day, advocating bias and hate-filled judgment on others, simply because of their race or religion. Nothing was gained by his life in the world.

Mankind should be aware that just as he would destroy an animal that preys upon people, he can also take a human life for the same reasons. Not out of hatred or spite, but in the wisdom and joint agreement that society cannot and should not support the lives of those men that devastate the lives of others. We don't mean to say that any man should become a vigilante or seek revenge against another, of course. That is why the judicial system exists. Judges are in place to protect the needs of society and there is no sin in removing a destructive and murderous person from the world. Giving such a person back to the light is the wisest answer in such cases.

The view that all life is invaluable is misguided. Not all lives or people are created equal, either physically or spiritually. But all are created by love and all return to love without fear of ever being the same again.

Murder

In speaking of morals and virtues, there are many wounds a man can impose on others. Let's have a look at murder, for example. Murder is a loveless act and goes against the nature of the soul's very design. Yet, the soul of a murderer is no different than that of a housewife in heaven's eyes. They have the same need to be loved, the same right to be loved here in our world. Though not all souls are created equal in mortal life, they are equal in this place. Although their needs differ from some, they are treated with the same love and kindness as the others.

On earth, society's laws don't always carry out justice. Some murderers are never caught, for example. Many people feel a need to see justice served, as it stabilizes their upturned world. But, justice or no justice, it is wiser for a person to accept the loss of a loved one, knowing that the one they have lost still lives on in a better place. The murderer's victim no longer suffers here and there is no more fear or terror in their new lives as souls.

The murderer is in the same position here as the suicidal soul. He must watch over all those who he's harmed in the world by his actions. He sees the consequences of his ungoverned, faithless actions. He must work to heal wounds – both the wounds he caused to others and the wounds within himself that caused him to hurt others. At the same time he tries to rise, he is being pulled downward and tugged by earthly grief and anger. The viewing gives murderers an awareness of just how senseless their lives had been and gives them a detached compassion for themselves as they once were, as well as for those they have hurt. Here, in this place, the light of love fills them. As it does, the greater the need they feel to give love to others. It is neither a justice system nor a reward system here. This place is for all mankind. Both lit souls and unlit, as well. It is your home. Here, there is only one thing compelling us and that is to fill all life with love. It is not an option. Love is all that exists here.

The murderer's victim does not suffer here because the body soon forgets pain. Any woman who has given birth to a child can attest to that, but once dead to the world there is no longer a body at all. In a soul's detachment from a body, the soul soon detaches from any memories of physical pain or suffering whatsoever. Think about it. Nerve endings are connected to the brain, right? Once the body dies, the soul no longer feels anything physical at all. With no ego, no body, no more need to process anything, and nothing to process it with, the soul is free to "just be" in its constant state of growing love.

When a soul arrives here, even after a sudden death, he is automatically detached from all things human. As he grows in light the "forgetting" is as effortless as the process of recording memories was in his worldly life. Because there is no longer a need to strive for physical survival, there is no need for anything to be recorded. You might be asking yourself "Well, if there's no need for memory in your world, what about the illusions that new souls are given there upon arrival?" So they are given, but a soul receives the illusion from those that wait to meet him and to serve him in his newness to eternity. The Wings that greet the new soul possess the enlightenment needed to clearly see what state the new soul has arrived in, as well as how his love in life has served him and how he has – or has not - served life.

The illusion is like a dream of happiness and not his reality. It fills the soul and soothes him. As the soul Lightens Up, the illusion begins to wane. This allows the soul to move forward here. In the case of a murderer, he begins to see how his selfish behavior and actions harmed not only his victim, but also everyone his actions affected, either directly or indirectly. He or she eventually learns to travel from place to place in order to overlook the living and share love with others there who need it. So, unlike other souls, the illusion the new soul is given is not quite a replica of his happiest days on earth. His illusion is not a little house with a dog and a fireplace, but is given to help him adjust to the shock of seeing how he lived his life and to ease the shock of his arrival in this place. The illusion is simply a cocoon of ever giving love that fills the gaps for the world-weary soul upon his/her arrival here.

Chapter Twelve

Wires of Love

The following chapters explain how the Wings would like to see us living life here on earth. Before we read that far, though, the Wings have written about something called "wires", which bridges our world with theirs and also connects each of us with our loved ones in this world. Because these wires do connect with both worlds and affect the way we live, it seems a good place to begin. I found the knowledge about the wires, which connect kindred spirits to one another, to be a very simple concept if you liken it to something with which most of us are already very familiar... email and the way the Internet works. include them with the "How To Live" section of this book, rather than include them in Part One, which describes life in the Wings' world.

Every person, every soul, is connected with others by wires, or conduits of love's energy. Each and every person's aura is unique and individual and the light that shines in your aura can be traced directly to you. These wires are made from lights of love that are small, but stretch very long distances to link souls. While old habits are hard to break, the connection between close friendships is even harder to break. Between the mutual affection of two souls, there are no miles separating them. There are just lines of light that flatten out into ribbons of color. These wires aren't just lines, but are the links we use to love others. It is not only one's thoughts about a person that passes through these wires, but it is the love shared between them. That's why people who are in your heart are forever with you, even after death. Even when they are not in your mind, they are always present in your love.

Love perpetuates itself by thickening the wires with more love and the wires that connect millions of souls in the world crisscross and color the entire planet. Although people cannot see these wires, the view from here above is fabulous and they are amazing to watch! The world, as seen from above, is hardly wide open at all, but is a sea of moving color, threading and entwining around the globe like a moving, colorful mass of light. There is no love that is untouched by that of another and no soul is ever truly alone. No soul is ever forgotten, regardless of the state of that soul, be it bright or dimly lit. Love wraps all souls in its light and the colors of love light up the world.

How many times have you turned away from a person because you can't be bothered connecting with them? Don't think that you have to adore everyone, as it is nearly impossible to love everyone you meet. There is no one that is not loved by someone, however; even it is only by us Wings. Things are not always as they seem and those that feel they are alone and forsaken in the world are not. Selfishness takes on new meaning when you think of it in terms of the wires that connect souls. A person who acts selfishly, thinking just of himself, only absorbs the wires of light, rather than both receiving and returning the flow of love within him or her. In doing so, they also hold onto their fears and sorrows, never releasing them. They close their hearts to the world and become prisoners of the wounds within them. The light of love flows like an endless river, but the current is meant to flow both ways. Acting in a self-centered or selfish manner halts the flow.

When this happens, the person's soul cannot thrive. It needs the flow of love going both in and out in order for a person to live happily and joyfully. Once you start blocking the flow of love, anything can happen and none of it is good. Love is like an endlessly filling well. It must flow constantly, as that is its nature. Cancel its destination and the soul begins to die of thirst. In doing so, the person's soul becomes darker and darker.

Some souls are born into the world with very little light within them, yet all are capable of growing lighter in life. For those that do, the rewards are infinite because they started out poor, so to speak, and became rich in love through their own efforts. Oftentimes these are souls that cannot be out in the world, due to mental or emotional problems that began in birth. Although they are at a great disadvantage in physical life because of their handicaps, the wires of love are always within them, as they are within all of us. Some use these wires to give without question and forge bonds of love with those around them. There is always love surrounding us, even in the darkest moment of life and in the hardest of circumstances we face. If the physically and mentally challenged can use these wires to connect with others and to Lighten Up their own souls, why can't you?

The answer is that you can, if you choose to do so. Imagine the wires of love within you like e-mailing your friends over the Internet. You might send and receive jokes and lighthearted messages with one person. That person passes it on to others, and the next person sends it on to others and others, as well, that are a long way from you. The message within the e-mail is the same. It remains unchanged, yet its origins are unknown to nearly everyone. It came to you and you passed it on. This is only some small joke, yet passing it along brightens and touches the lives of many others, reaffirming friendships and strengthening the bonds between people.

The wires of love that connect peoples' souls work exactly the same way. You are created by love and move through the world giving of yourself, whether it's your skills, money, or deeds. However you look at life, it is about flow. When a person locks himself or herself away from the world, whether it is in actual physical terms or by emotional withdrawal, everyone in the world is affected in some way. For example, people that depend upon you to pay your bills or have contacted you to provide them with a service are affected by your actions. For some, your absence is a nuisance, while for others it's a worry.

But, in breaking the "give and take" of yourself, you cause a chain reaction that either creates or blocks a flow of love to other souls, affecting them in a beneficial or adverse way.

To starve the soul of love by your own selfish actions creates illness and bad effect for all. If a person hides away from love, it becomes easier for them to act in a loveless way. This, in turn, affects society as a whole, opening the door to things like anti-social and criminal behavior. A chain reaction results, affecting everyone this person meets, which affects everyone they meet and so on. The greater a person starves his soul through withholding love for others, and only taking from it, the more he becomes a wounding part of the world as a whole. The reason we could never judge or punish such a soul upon his arrival here in the afterlife is because to do so would be to withhold the very thing he or she most needs. While it's true that these souls acted badly in their lives, living in darkness and harming many with their selfish behavior, we cannot teach them a lesson by withholding the very thing they most need to understand. Which is, of course, learning how to give love.

Love's nature is to flow. It is never repelled by darkness. It is not some weak little flicker of light to be dimmed or snuffed out by a mortal's dark soul. Love is an illumination greater than a billion suns. It knows no fear, as fear is the opposite of love. It is whole, pure, enormous and ever growing. Love is alive and ultimately overpowers all. There is no person and no thing that can have any effect on it. To understand this truth removes fear, sorrow or any other negative human emotion.

When people die and arrive into the true glory of their life here, they are both overjoyed and overpowered by the light of love they discover. When they are given the viewing of their worldly lives, as we have discussed elsewhere in this book, they are able to perceive with their own awareness these wires that we discuss here. They are able to see the most amazing sight of love that fills the spaces between people. It is truly overwhelming and humbling for the soul to view. They see the lines of love that stretch to them from all the people they touched in life. While you might expect it from some, such as your wife or family, you don't expect to see it from so many people you don't know or have never even met. It is the way your wires connect with the people you affected in life – directly or indirectly, good or bad - that determines how you will live your life here in the next world.

We want people to know that all they need in life is already within them. It is love and it flows in and out with everything they do, say, and think. The way to a simpler and more joy-filled life is to simply believe in the light that the person standing next to you shines from within him or her. Yes, there are plenty of unlit, dark souls in the world to be avoided, as it is not safe to act like a simple child in a dangerous world. But you can find the balance of giving wisely to others and to yourself.

Don't stop giving love. Don't limit your love by thinking, "Well, I'll love only those that love me or just those that are kind to me." Give your love generously and you will see it returned to you one hundred times over. Use love like the air you breathe and it will flow within you like air does. Walk around imagining the very real fog of love's light that fills every space. Visualize the wires and ribbons of light that link us and pass through us from one to the other. These wires are more real and far larger than you can imagine.

Look at the furniture in your rooms, the foods you eat, the things taken for granted. Consider that they were once someone's idea and someone worked hard using the love within them to make them a reality for everyone to enjoy. Stop and think how many wires of love are bound together and connected in every little thing you see, smell, taste and feel. Life is not only what it appears to be in the world around you. Life is an enormous soup and we are all part of this soup. It is the soup that sustains life.

Murder and other hideous crimes are so painful because they block the lines of love within us. But the death of a person doesn't stop love from flowing through other wires, nor does it stop the creation of new wires as a result of the dark soul's actions. Love simply exists, and it never dies. It continues to grow and love conquers all, just as the saying goes. It's always present. It's simply that humans lack the perception to see the wires of love. Just because you can't see them doesn't mean they don't exist, however. Can you see the air that you breathe?

We say that you should use faith as your guide to living. Believe in what you now know to be true. That, of course, is that the love within you, whether expressed as a parent, a friend, or the courtesy given to a stranger, is what makes life go round.

When people are slowly dying, the wires of love within them become more of a one-way flow, rather than a give and take flow. The dying human has love flowing into them, but as their hold on life weakens they aren't able to return as much as they receive. They become like sponges of love and when the soul becomes filled with love, they pass over. Every soul has a different amount of love he receives during this time. Some need little when they arrive here, as they came with a lot of love within them upon their arrival. A Wing arrives here as a well lit soul and gives a lot of joy to other souls here. Although some earthbound Wings do live long lives, they do not have to live very long lives because they are easily topped off to saturation. Remember that a Wing comes to earth to answer a call of love. Their wires are already loaded with much love before they arrive on earth. Once his job is done, he is no longer needed on earth, so he is called home.

There is no hard and fast rule about living as a mortal and there is no easy way to understand how wires are used to guide human lives. Nor is it easy to understand how someone that seems to be a perfect stranger can kill another without motive. Some things are beyond human understanding. One that all of you can understand, however, is a very simple concept and that is learning to live with the awareness of love on both a personal and a universal scale.

Once people begin to understand just how many others they affect on an hourly basis... just how important their actions are to people they aren't even aware of, they are then able to start living within the light of love. Once they're aware of this knowledge, they cannot ever live blindly again. When people understand that love is the reason they exist, and not the other way around, it is something they can never forget. And knowing that your soul returns to the place of pure love upon death is what everyone wishes for in life. Like anything, the more you invest in something, the more you get out of it. In this case, the more faith and love you invest, the more you get out of life, both before and after death.

Wires are the physical links of love between people, joining one love to another. The wires are many and some people have so many wires connecting them with others that they are beyond count. Wires do not govern your life, nor guide you through life. It's quite the opposite. The way you live governs them.

Chapter Thirteen

Faith and Acceptance

The souls assure us that faith and acceptance are the two most important principles we can learn in life, if we want to live happily and begin to Lighten Up as souls before we leave this world. Faith and acceptance, or acceptance and faith, are intertwined as key elements of a worthwhile life. If we have faith that life is never ending, it makes accepting heartache and other challenging situations far less difficult. Not always easy, but definitely less difficult.

One of the perks of writing books is that you can

include a shameless plug about yourself if you feel like it. The first paragraph in this chapter is mine. It proves my ego is still intact, at least to a degree, which just goes to show I'm no angel. The good news is that the swelling has gone down considerably since my drinking days, greatly reducing a once fragile, badly bloated ego. As a result, most of my fears have largely diminished, as well, including the fear of criticism.

We wish to talk about faith today. Let's start with the way Danny lives. He hasn't a frightened bone in his body. Assisting us, as he does, to fulfill the book is the way he learns and allows our words to be written. This is great for all of us in this plan to touch others. The plan has always been to write the book, but we allow him the plot that is worded with him in mind. His talents can pat it into a lovely cake. Thinking about us is a ray of sunshine for him as it sits innocently out there in the light of awakening and enlightenment. Angels at his table are a witness to his need for reaffirmation and God's willingness to love.

People are used to turning life into an event or a multitude of events that must be struggled with and overcome. Thinking that everything is an obstacle that must be "dealt with" is the main source of anger and tension for many people. Naturally, with so many people all going about their daily business, there are bound to be countless events that a person must deal with in his daily life. The trick is to simply recognize that you, like them, are not all living each moment like automatons (a word to describe a self-operating machine invented in 1739, interestingly enough). You are active appreciators of being one small part of a very large system.

Faith is like the glue that holds people and situations together when it seems everything is falling apart. Faith is unlimited by anything other than the person that possesses it. Faith might not move mountains, but faith creates.

Creates? you ask. Why, yes, we reply. It is not what you do in life, but how you give to it that ensures the best outcome. To live one's life in the assuredness that love is the most important thing, for example, allows love to flow freely. Life is all about love. Faith opens the door to allow love to flow to you and from you to others. We Wings can work love to your best advantage by passing it through others, either from or to you. Love is a giving thing by its very nature and is best expressed through the connections you create in life. Faith is like having green lights all the way. The first green light you pass through is good, the second one is great, and the third is both exhilarating and calming at the same time. The driver is aware that the way forward is made easy, which is unusual and rewarding in itself.

Of course, no one wants to be late for work while stuck on a highway through no fault of his or her own. And here is a perfect example of how to live life with faith. In such a scenario, you can react in very different ways. The next time it happens to you, stop for a moment and examine what is happening with your mind and body. You might feel exasperated and impatient, your anger growing as your mind starts its ceaseless turning of wheels. Your brain creates images of the potential consequences of being held up in traffic, both for your benefit and for your viewing displeasure. Your thoughts tell you that the whole trip will probably be slow once traffic begins moving again, if it moves at all, and that more stop and go traffic will be likely. It means you won't have time for that extra cup of coffee, all the good parking spots will be taken, and you'll be late for work, which won't please your boss or your clients.

The list of potential problems is endless, of course, and the level of tension your mind has created leaves no room for anything else as it forces your body to respond to its speed of light connections. You are struggling against some small "event" that has assumed enormous proportions in your mind. Your whole day will be ruined now as you present your less-than-happy face and dark aura to those you come in contact with; not only in your physical contacts, but your spiritual ones, as well. When this happens, love faces a roadblock of negativity and it cannot flow from us to you or from you to others. This type of reaction to the traffic jams of life is a learned one and the best way to begin unlearning it is to become aware that it is happening to you.

Let's look at the same situation again. Those of you who have faith realize that there will be these little "hold ups" from time to time. The faithful understand that it's part of the deal when traveling a busy highway. So, you take the time to have your coffee before you leave the house in the morning and you leave a little earlier, too. You also know that there are some really big problems in the world and that this is not one of them. Faith is telling yourself "I'll deal with things as they come and all will be well." You take a deep breath, relax, and choose to enjoy the moment.

Faith is not something that demands prayer on bended knee every morning before walking out the door. Possessing faith in one's life simply allows you to see that as a bit player in a very large play called life, you can do your part in it to the best of your ability by making things a little easier to deal with in your own life. When you learn to handle things in your own life a little easier, it can't help but make life a little easier for others. It means you don't become so agitated that you begin counting the times you've done some task for a friend or family member, nor denying them the love you can give them through your faith. You have faith in them, faith in yourself, and faith in life. Faith is the door through which love flows in and out of you. It smoothes out the small problems in life, which, in turn, make the big picture known as living a much nicer thing.

Those with faith know that no matter how long it takes the traffic will begin moving again. If you have to pay for a parking garage instead of slipping into your usual free spot, so what? No two days are ever quite the same and, in faith, you accept it. Fuming and complaining about it will not change things. Glaring at others will only make the situation worse. Should the worst happen and you die at the wheel, guess what happens next? Those with faith already know the answer. You return home to the world of light and love, where eternal joy awaits you with open arms. So what's the problem?

This knowledge, or faith, allows you to appreciate the many variables that every new day has to offer. You can count on the "traffic jams of life" to happen. Make allowances for them and learn to accept them as part of life. You'll make everyone's life a better place if you do. Your smile, the light that shines from within you, touches everyone in both worlds. People understand you always do your best in a relaxed and giving way and life flows for you like those three or four green lights we discussed. People will give to you because you go with the flow of life and don't try to "deal" with it.

Faith is not a religious doctrine, nor a thing that only saints possess. Faith is living in the fullness of your love. Faith is being aware that there is more to life than traffic or taxes or the senseless cruelty of others. Faith is your willingness to go through a day without pouting because you are not the star player in this mega-production called life. You understand that the world doesn't revolve around any of us and you feel grateful to be a part of life. Faith is the knowledge that little things and large things will happen, just as surely as you will die one day or grow wrinkled. Faith allows you to accept that life is about giving and receiving love from others – both living in the world and outside of it. That is, after all, what you were designed to do in the first place. Simply that.

Faith won't necessarily cure cancer or help you win the lottery, but with it you can accept in the most graceful fashion that this life you are living will one day be replaced with another life so much richer than this one, that there are no words to describe it. Whether those you love are taken from the earth, be it through illness or by the hands of another, doesn't matter in the grand scheme of things. They still live in their truest form when they arrive here, filling themselves and others with the light of love. There is no use in pretending that loving only those who give you love is the right way to live. Loving in such a way is self-defeating and limiting. Love cannot live alone. It is social in nature, as are you, and believes the more, the merrier! Throw love out there and it not only returns to you, but also brings more love with it.

Let's talk about the best way to express faith. You might not have any money left over at the end of the week, but you can still extend a smile or a few kind words to another, be it your neighbor, a store cashier, or someone you pass on the street. It costs nothing and it is truly appreciated by others. Not always because it came from you, personally, but just because it came. Not every person you meet is going to like you for it or appreciate your offer of kindness. But, they become part of a chain reaction, whether they are aware of it or not. You might not even like the person very much, but that is not the point. Love flows to love, period. The key to love is faith in your own life and faith in others, as well. Not blind trust in someone who might appear dangerous, of course, but living in faith allows you to move safer within your world because it is a way for people to accept one another. Yet, acceptance is the one thing that gives people the most trouble.

There is no need to analyze acceptance, nor become "one with it". There is also, however, no weakness in discovering and applying acceptance in our lives. We are not just talking about accepting people here, but the other inevitable things in life, as well. People find it nearly impossible to accept the death of a loved one, especially when the death is very sudden or involves the murder or accidental death of a loved one. To accept someone's viciousness in taking the life of one we love seems like a betrayal of the loved one. Understandably, the mourner usually focuses on trying to find a reason why it happened or questions why one person would kill another. Failing to understand, the tendency is then to want revenge, thinking that harsh justice will bring us "closure" and some kind of peace once the murderer has been executed.

Yet, should the killer be put to death or hidden away from

society in prison, there is still no real soothing of the grief the mourner feels afterward. Grief is about loss. It is the loss of your own expression of love to another and the loss of the joy that person gave to you. There is absolutely nothing in revenge that can soothe such a loss. Your ego cannot simply dust itself off after getting back up off the ground. It has been crippled by the loss of its ability to express itself. There is nothing one can do to make it go away. There is, however, one way to learn to live a full life again, and that is through acceptance. Time is not the healer and, contrary to popular belief, time does not heal all wounds. The dead remain dead to the people they've left behind. They still died in the same way, no matter how much time has passed. A person who has faith, however, finds acceptance easier than those without faith. He knows that his loved one still lives on in a better place. It doesn't mean he doesn't miss his loved one, but he understands that the murderer killed no one, in reality, or that the suicide victim is not really dead at all, but is surrounded by the love of others.

Faith offers a depth of acceptance that allows love to flow during both pleasant and horrible times alike. By applying faith, you create more of it. In creating more, your life becomes richer because you are at one with yourself and one with your world. Life is guaranteed to have its bad times and you can count on them. Faith is the "insurance policy" that these times will pass and these bad times do no injury to a person's soul; bodily harm, maybe, and emotional pain, certainly, but no harm ever comes to your soul. The soul can only be wounded by your lack of faith that life is never ending and by your refusal to believe that love is where you came from and where you will return again.

Should a person become so darkly colored (aura) that his life is no longer livable, it is because his faith has been withheld and ignored. So what can a person do to awaken his faith? Practice putting faith into everything you do in life. Start in small ways. Do an ordinary daily task like making coffee in the morning and asking someone if they would like to join you. Take pleasure in the moment, knowing that you are making another person's life a little nicer. It's these small moments of kindness that grow into larger things. Massage and nurture your faith by understanding you have extended yourself to another in love, regardless of whether they ignored you, snapped at you, or accepted your invitation. In this most simple act and extension of yourself, you have acted in faith. You have used faith and you literally feel lighter because of it. So easy to do and so often ignored. Yet, the more you extend yourself through your personality, the more things happen for you. Little things come along to ease your life. Not breathtaking things, perhaps, but things that smooth the road ahead of you. Love cannot stop itself once it begins to flow. It must keep going by its very nature. Even when it hits a blocked soul it will push on in any way it is able and is never wasted. Believe in love. Have faith in its power to flow both from and to you.

There are very few people without any faith at all, whether or not they are aware of it. A missing child shakes a parent to the marrow of their bones. But even as they are living in their worst nightmare, they are putting their faith into the police, the community and sometimes, even psychics to assist them and reveal the truth. It is in these moments that one's soul reels the most. In moments like these, the sheer horror cannot be easily overcome. Faith, however, reminds us that love is real and life is eternal, even if we can't always see it as humans. Faith assures us that the horrors of death, even of a child, are forgotten in the moment of death. To remember these things is to live in faith. It is the reason we want you to know we exist.

We urge people to have faith so that all on earth can live in joy sooner, rather than later. Use faith to repair yourselves, others, and the world in which you live. Faith costs nothing and pays off in so many ways. What more can you ask for than that? Using faith to spread the lightness of your being is the reason you were created, not to earn a million dollars or break your back making your life one big, difficult "event" to be "dealt with". The only true challenge in life is remembering that you are a child of the light and that living human lives allows you to "graduate", regardless of whether you learned the lesson you came to study or even remember what it is you are here to learn. You all pass the test. How can you ever fail when you become one with love?

We'd like to add one more thing about faith. Those that do nothing to their best abilities in life and only call on God when they are at a low point in their life cannot hope to find an answer to their prayer. Appreciating life and making sure to act wholeheartedly in all we do is the key to receiving help from God. Remember that faith is the key that unlocks the door to love and joy and invites them into our lives. You must meet them halfway. If you act like a spoiled child that wants gifts from his parents, but doesn't want to help out around the house, then you reap as you sow. The child that plays nice and does his chores without looking for anything but the love of his parents is the child that receives the best gifts.

We will all suffer wounds at some point in our lives. Some people, like a child born into an abusive or loveless home, carry wounds from birth. We will do all we can to help the child move beyond this wound. As the child grows, he can choose to hold onto his wounds, never getting past them, or he can strive to give more love than he was given in life. In applying faith, he has chosen not to "hit back" at the world, but to rise above the occasion. Once we learn to apply faith in our daily lives, we forget about the limitations the card deck of life dealt us and we learn to rise above them.

The more faith you can raise within yourself, the easier and more beautiful your life will become. Faith is so easy to apply. It just means taking a moment to appreciate that an event or understanding that a moment that troubles you is just that... a moment. The hurt, the tears, fears, or any of the things that wrack your bodies and minds are simply moments. They are passages that lead to a love far greater than a parent feels for his child, if you choose to apply them using faith.

Despite the things that feel like forever in one's life, a lifetime is so fleeting, in reality. We all know how slowly time seems to pass when we are in a place or situation we dislike, and how time flies when we're having a fun time. Faith feeds a person's soul while helping to make all given situations move faster. Yes, even the worst time will pass more quickly if love flows through you. Faith is the key to the lock. It opens the door to love.

In the joy of running in life, people trip, fall, and get the stitch (surgical stitches). They collapse, stagger, finish in third place or even finish last. It doesn't matter at all. The point is that they ran! That's important to know. It's not the outcome that matters, so much, as the act of living with faith and love that's important. There is an expression people like to say in your world. "Wake up and smell the coffee." It is a perfect example of living life in awareness of faith and love.

Can you see how simple life is? There is no effort if you subtract the fear of failure or looking foolish from the equation. There is nothing to fear in living the way you were designed to live, which is living your life with the same willingness as your body works the engine of itself. Both are designed to go and go. Your body works because that is its purpose in life. What is your purpose? It's to live in love and faith. The psyche of a man is the same as the body. Both are designed to live in willingness and to experience all it is able.

To accept the wound you chose to carry in the world is to acknowledge that love has its wisdom. Accepting this truth minimizes the wounds one feels and helps you to rise above problems and move forward in life. Think of the abused woman. She might have been physically beaten, verbally abused, or perhaps forced to suffer the loss of her baby at the hands of another through miscarriage or forced to abort life. For those without faith in the power of love, such a woman might lose her will to live. If she uses faith to rise above herself and her problems, however, she will find that the power of love will assist her. This is the essence of living. Love assists life.

But, one might ask, what about the baby's suffering?

Remember that suffering is forgotten at death and is replaced by the joy of reuniting with whole love, here in the next life. Remember also the joy the woman felt in creating and carrying the child's love within her and the joy it had created. Focus on that, not the wound the abuse had created. It's also important to remember that excessive grief holds the child in its dark grip and that grief carried too long is a selfish thing that is more about "poor me" more than anything else. Most of all, remember that life on earth is only a part time job and not a full time existence. Even the mourner will find himself in pure love again after death and will become light and joyful once again. But those that lived without faith will have to work off the dark images they carry within them when they arrive here. It is not faithless or disloyal to let go of grief. Grief is like an illness, in that it gradually begins to lessen. Using faith, it lessens a little more, and then a little more, until one day you are well again. This is faith and love at its finest. The way to ease this passing cloud is to focus on the joy of living and not on the sorrow-filled end of a loved one's life.

Each person has the ability to re-direct his or her feelings into a positive direction. You can choose to rise above mental, emotional and physical abuse. You can decide to re-direct personal feelings of loss and rage into a social direction that will have a positive effect in the world. Use faith and love to create joy, rather than using negativity and self-centered behavior to destroy it. Don't allow yourself to become a prisoner to those people that have harmed you in life. Why give them the power to control your happiness when it is within you to enjoy? Instead, reclaim the joy of living that is not only your right to embrace, but also an obligation. For the soul that caused this grief through his own unwillingness to embrace life, he will have to pay by society's standards on earth and he will have to work much harder to Lighten Up in this place than most. The only way he can makes amends to those he hurts is to learn faith. Respecting others is not easy for the unlit soul.

There will always be those that create suffering. This is a part of life in its most basic form. But Wings are living examples of how to rise above their circumstances, both literally and figuratively. By living out their lives using daily expressions of love, they can give more to the world than the unlit can ever take away.

If a person strives hard to do everything right and still finds no reward, they are overlooking something within themselves that is blocking the flow of love to and from them. In order to open yourself to love, you must be aware when you find yourself plodding along in life. Not every job or act we do is a joyful one, but the way you approach it from within you makes all the difference. Much is written about visualizing things in life. It is true that if you do any ordinary task with the image of a happy outcome, be it washing dishes, planting a crop, or designing a building, then good effect will follow for you in life.

The crop you plant out of love inspires others to plant their own seeds. Love provides work for others, food on tables, and goods in shops to be happily bought and enjoyed by many. It is an example that everything in life is a product of giving. The reason man began saying grace before meals was to give awareness and appreciation to the love that nourishes souls. Once people start using loving awareness toward all things, life becomes richer and more fulfilling. Life then flows liquidly, just as love itself flows. Living happily is as simple as smiling with your eyes into the eyes of another or taking a moment to give praise or appreciation for their efforts. You all know how it feels to be the recipient of appreciation. It lightens the moment and brightens your day. This is what it means to Lighten Up. Life needs the same appreciation as people and, in turn, gives the same back to you.

A weed pulled out of a pathway doesn't take but a moment. Yet, when done daily you are creating a lovely clear path, which pleases others. At the same time, you avoid the gigantic chore, anxiety, and criticism that result if you let it become overgrown for months at a time. If you pay someone else to do it for you, you deny yourself the appreciation you could be feeling yourself in maintaining and preserving your own sense of value and appreciation for having done the job yourself. Whatever you do in life, do it with full happiness. Focus on things like your ability to be able to do it and your awareness of why you are doing it and think of the ripple effect it has on others... and others and others. Even small sounds create ripples on the water. So much goes into the creation of a human being. The creation process has so much involved in it, yet it happens effortlessly. Love does the same, given the chance.

Here in the light, we often look at our old lives. Although we love reflecting upon our own past lives nostalgically, our hearts just aren't in it anymore. We see those who think of us and we overlook their lives. We know that they are all right, even when their lives seem to be crashing down around them. That is not the case, however, as life and love are never ending and everything that happens in life is meant to be. We are all given lessons to learn in order to rise above life's obstacles. This is the reason why people seldom hear an answer to their prayers and it's the reason we say praying in any other way than to thank God for life is a waste of time. Prayer is important in life, but must be done through faith that whatever happens to us in worldly life will mean little once our physical lives have ended. Life will always be a harsh ruler, with its many degrees of pleasure and pain. There are always ups and downs in the whole deal of living. .

The trick is to live as wisely as possible, remembering that it is up to you to make your own way in life. It's your responsibility to remember that there is a consequence to everything we do in life. The more you live with this awareness, the easier life becomes for you and others, as well.

These days, the direction many people follow is the "just do it" philosophy. In some cases, this is good advice, especially when we are afraid to take a step into the unknown. It is a step of faith. If you repeatedly skin your shin as you take that step, then you'll know that step needs retracting and a new direction is needed. Life is about choices. How you react to the downs of life, as well as the ups. How you move forward, or not, is your choice and yours alone.

There are always ways and means available to move

forward in life. It is up to each person to have enough faith to choose to use them. In today's "hurry up", rush and scurry world, people often play too many roles. People feel pressured to rush into decisions. This creates a forced pace of life, not a natural and joyous one. In earlier times, no one had to make decisions as quickly as people feel compelled to do these days. There is so much pressure in life now, be it on the road or in one's heart. People live very different and difficult lives today, but that is only through their own choices. Even opting out of the rat race requires huge decisions and complex interactions. Nothing is ever easy anymore.

Yet, if you use faith and love as your guide, you grease the wheels. This, however, does not happen overnight. In order for love to flow freely and make life a happier and freer thing, you must start the wheels turning by using all the generosity of your human heart. This goes against the nature of the human mind, which is always on the lookout for its own interests. Think with your heart, as well as your mind, and give your best in all you do.

Living here in the light is a fine thing, indeed. There is nothing like it. WE WANT PEOPLE TO KNOW THAT DEATH IS GREAT! HEAVENLY! WONDROUS! Living in this place is simply beyond words. Can you imagine not having a single care? Never feeling tired or weary? Never finding yourself alone in your heart and feeling totally and purely loved throughout every tiny, micro particle of yourself. There is no way to explain just how filling the light within us truly feels. It is more than filling, it is us and it will be you one day. This life is not something we discuss or debate and there are no laws here to obey. No restrictions, whatsoever. Life in the light is total freedom of both time and space. We can leave and return anytime we choose. Life here is knowing all and seeing all. Quite simply, all is love!

We have said in this book that there are lit and unlit souls. We also say that there is no difference between the two in this place of love and light. There is no segregation and there are no limits for either. Unlit can become lit and the lit souls can go on to become more luminous. It is a choice for all. Our wish for man is that he will learn from this book and will shout in joy, "I AM ALIVE AND I GIVE LOVE!" Naturally, more than a few people only take from love, but never forget – and this is especially important for those that are still wounded by life – THE CHOICE IS ALWAYS YOURS! Whether lit or unlit, you only have one choice in the end, and that is to be enveloped by love and light. Why not choose to Lighten Up now?

You dark souls who read these words cannot escape from light and love. You are not going to hell, nor are you sending anyone there. You must enter into the light upon your death. There is no hall pass, no excuse, no way out. No matter what you make of your life, no matter how you treat others or yourself, you will be loved and you will discover the true meaning of life and love. The two are one and the same. They are inseparable. We laugh in the joy of knowing it. Even the darkest soul receives what it needs here, which is pure love and pure light and even the lightest earthly soul thrills in receiving even more light.

Fear nothing. Not people, not death, not those that deliver death. Don't mourn too hard for loved ones lost. It is your loss you grieve, not theirs. Don't destroy your life by living in fear, as so many do. There is no need. There is everything for everyone here, a total carte blanche. The need of your soul is for the light of love and in death we find it naturally and easily. Life is an eternal cycle for all souls and all things.

Preaching to people is not our thing. We want the people of the world to simply understand that there is so much more joy in life than is ever seen in our physical lives. Many people will find the idea of man being created from light to be a very controversial subject. Read the following words, though, and tell me where the true argument is against our words. There is none. We say that all humans are born from light, but some souls contain more light than others and there are even some born with no soul at all. As you know, some humans are born into the world more fortunate than others, both physically and in the lifestyle they inherit. In every litter of puppies, some are born larger and stronger than others. The same is true for man. Yet, you are all human.

Your happiness or misery stems from one of two things – allowing love to flow from you and to you, or a blockage of love within you.

Faith is the key that opens the door to your heart and allows love and light to flow to you. You have the power to apply faith and giving in all you do or you can remain locked behind the door, too afraid to step outside. The choice is yours. That is life in a nutshell.

Chapter Fourteen

Lighten Up, Will You?

Apart from brief chapter introductions like this one, I let the Seven Soul Writers do all the talking in the first thirteen chapters. This chapter is where I've added my two cents, for what it's worth. Welcome back to Planet Earth!

Have I told you about the fifteen years I spent crawling on tile floors, removing and replacing the rock hard, cement-based material between tiles known as grout? The work is every bit as fascinating as it sounds. My new job as the grout guy began at age 40, shortly after retiring from my previous 20-year stint as a restless, cynical, hardcore alcoholic.

Having walked on both sides of the grout fence, I can tell you there are two ways you can approach this type of work.

You can moan and groan about your upcoming day before you even get out of bed in the morning. This is a highly effective way of ruining your day and your family's morning, as well. You can also force your fellow drivers to bear the brunt of your displeasure on the way to work by tailgating, hogging lanes and refusing to yield in traffic. Misery loves company, after all. Once you start work, be sure to spend the entire time you're scraping grout wishing you were somewhere else, while cursing under your breath for good measure. When you finally arrive home at the end of the day, be sure to complain about your hellish day to anyone within earshot. Don't forget to vent your frustration towards the wife and kids, and even the family dog. This will ensure your efforts to ruin their day earlier haven't been a

Chapter Fourteen - Lighten Up, Will You?

failure. But don't limit yourself to sharing your misery with family members or other drivers. Why pass up the opportunity to infect everyone else you meet with your negativity, as well? Whether it's your co-workers, neighbors, or the convenience store employee you meet while heading to or from work. As an added bonus, allow yourself the luxury of self-pity, asking why you've been dealt such a lousy hand by the card deck of life. Be sure to feel sorry for yourself each and every day and don't fail to ask why God wants to punish you. If God even exists, that is. How could there be one, now that you think about it? After all, no caring, loving God would ever allow you to be so miserable, right? These are some truly effective techniques guaranteed to make you feel special and unique. There is no better way to separate you from the idiots of the world. Well done, ego! Bravo!

Some might think that the above scenario doesn't apply to them because they never scream at the kids, keep their mouths shut, and always drive safely. Those people aren't off the

229

hook, though, unless they are giving love to others every day. It's not enough to simply keep your head down and mind your own business. No more than a forced, phony smile is enough to replace a warm, genuine grin.

The other way you can approach grout work is by choosing to apply acceptance, gratitude and faith. You can be grateful to have two arms and two legs to do the job with, for starters. Some people don't have all their limbs. Others do, but sit paralyzed in a wheelchair, unable to use them. I wonder what those people would give to trade places with the grout man?

You can also use your faith, knowing that whatever task we do to make someone's life a little better, no matter how small, is an important expression of love. Many a housewife's face lights up when she sees how you've transformed her once ugly, black, moldy shower into something beautiful. She no longer has to spend hours with a toothbrush and a bottle of bleach struggling to get it clean. The housewife, in turn, touches others with her happiness and appreciation for a job well done. The grout man has given her his best and she passes along her best to others, as a natural result. It's through the little things that love flows in the world.

You can also choose to accept that the work is challenging and rise to the challenge, using faith in your ability to do the job well. You can use faith, acceptance and gratitude all at once if you choose to view life as a never-ending gift of love and feel grateful for your part in it, knowing this gift is yours to be expressed and enjoyed in all you do.

The moral of the story is that we can choose to apply joy and love in all we do, whether it's scraping grout, cleaning the oven, or sunbathing on a tropical island. Or we can sit around cursing the world for not revolving around us. Believe it or not, some people are no happier soaking up the sun in Hawaii than they would be scrubbing a septic tank in a ghetto. Wherever you go, you always take you along for the ride.

You can substitute the words "difficult task" with difficult people or difficult situations, such as your car breaking down fifty miles east of nowhere or the way you react to the next rude person you run into at the supermarket. Accepting the challenges in life, as well as the perks, completely changes how we approach the "grout jobs" of life. Faith is the key to acceptance. As the Wings out it, faith and acceptance oil the wheels of life and make everything run a little smoother.

Marvin Gaye sang "only love can conquer hate". He was right. I don't know about you, but I'm not too wild about the state of affairs in today's world and have no intention of letting the unlit souls, many of whom are our so-called leaders, ruin things for the rest of us. You don't fight fire with fire, though, and negativity only breeds more of the same. Promote love and kindness to others in every little thing you do if you want to conquer hatred. Don't fool yourself into thinking that the way we feel inside doesn't affect the world as a whole. Both positive and negative thoughts are very real forms of energy. Much like a virus, holding back on love affects everyone we touch in some shape or form and everyone they meet, as well. Some are infected by negativity immediately, while others are unsuspecting carriers, passing the virus along to others. Faster than you can say the word re-grout, the negative energy we passed along to the convenience store employee on the way home from work in California has been passed along to the truck driver heading to Boston. That same truck driver will stop at least three times during the trip, passing the negativity virus on to God knows how many others.

Imagine how many people the truck driver might have filled with joy if you had shared a kind word or a smile with that convenience store employee on your ride home from work. Don't believe it's as simple as that? We'll never know if we never try.

You might ask "Who the hell died and made you an expert on life, Dan Farish?" Well, I used to be a big follower of the

Three Stooges, but it probably wasn't them. The true experts are the Seven Souls Writers of this book who died and lived to tell about it. A quote by an unknown author describes my role in this book. "God doesn't call the qualified. He qualifies the called." Whether or not you believe the Seven Writers still live on as souls plays a huge role in how you choose to live your life. For what it's worth, I've lived on both sides of the fence and was the poster boy for how not to live for most of my life. As a raging alcoholic and general malcontent for more than twenty years, my disconnection from love and spirit ran far deeper than your average Joe's. In other words, my main qualification for advising others how to live comes from decades of doing more stupid stuff than most.

The Seven Writers could just as easily have contacted someone far more qualified for the job, like Stephen King or Danielle Steele. You know, some world famous, guaranteed New York Times bestseller author with real clout and real talent. While it would be nice to convince myself that I'm somehow even more special and talented, the truth is that it's my less-than-pristine past that qualifies me for the task. It was the twenty years of faithless, empty living that drove my urge to drink. It was hitting bottom, as they say in addiction recovery, which is just what it sounds like. Your world crumbles around you, the gutter looks like up, and you're forced to choose between life and death. You're so lost in yourself and your addiction that those of us that do manage to crawl out of the hole only make it by reaching for a helping hand. In the case of many addicts, that helping hand comes from putting faith in a higher power. Our own power is about as sturdy as a wet paper bag by the time we reach for that hand.

I walked, talked and functioned on a basic human level, but did all three with the dimmer switch of my soul set to its lowest possible setting. I existed, but did not live. The faith and acceptance the Seven Souls discuss were the keys to turning the light on again. Both played major roles in receiving the intense spiritual experience that removed the overwhelming urge to drink 19 years ago. I had to accept that my addiction was stronger than me and had to have faith that a power greater than my own could, and would, help me if I asked.

Did the experience turn me into Sammy Sunshine?

Did I leap out of bed the next morning, jumping for joy? You would think so, after divine intervention stepped in and snatched me from falling deeper into the black pit of addiction. But that's not what happened. As mentioned above, I spent a year and a half hating grout, hating life and hating dragging myself out of bed in the morning, even after the spiritual experience. What the spiritual experience did do was remove the overwhelming urge to drink that held me firmly by the throat for two decades. I still had to learn to live happily.

A higher power answered my call for help when I was down and out. The energy that flowed through me consisted of pure, divine love. I touched it, inhaled it, and tasted it. This higher power was my soul group reaching out to one of their own. We share a connection that precedes birth, remains to this day, and continues to grow stronger. The spiritual connection that removed my addiction was just the beginning, however. Much like planting a seed, it first has to take root and start to sprout before it grows larger. In other words, I still had a lot of learning to do and will be learning until my number comes up and calls me back home, to the other side of life. Once the love that comes with a spiritual awakening begins to take root and grow, though, it never stops blossoming and expanding.

As the mental fog of addiction slowly lifted in the months and years that follow, most addicts and alcoholics not only learn to start living life, but make living happily their mission. We've missed out on a lot and want to make up for lost time. We learn to appreciate the simple things in life that most non-addicts take for granted. Rehabs and recovery groups have taught us the true meaning of the words the Wings speak of in this book. Words like faith and acceptance click with us, because we had to apply them in order to survive when we hit bottom. We are the fortunate ones. Our soul group members answered our call for help when we most needed it and we learned something about the value of life in the process. The wires of love that connect us are unbreakable and they are eternal. This is the reason they asked me to help write the book.

One day, not all that long ago, the ball finally dropped all the way. It was that day, after more than half a century of arriving in this world, that I truly learned to understand how to enjoy this thing called life. It was as easy as flicking on a light switch. Coincidentally (or not), it wasn't until I applied the same acceptance, faith and gratitude that the Wings speak of in this book that I began to grasp the concept of living in the way they suggest. By coincidentally, I mean they just happen to be the same words we were taught in addiction rehab, as discussed above. I understood these words to an extent, but never truly applied them in the simple way the souls explain it. And applying them was every bit as simple as the Wings assure us. It was as simple as choosing to smile at someone passing by in the grocery aisle or offering a few cheerful words to the cashier at the local convenience store. Even when some people don't appreciate our kindness, we are still sharing love and expressing ourselves as we are meant to live. That is the point of the exercise - nothing more and nothing less.

One challenge for any author is to remain objective while writing a non-fiction book. This is especially true while writing on someone else's behalf, which was the case with the Seven Soul Writers. As mentioned earlier, I limited my own comments earlier in this book in order not to lead you, the reader, astray with my own thoughts and opinions. This chapter is written solely from my own perspective, based on personal experience, using my own words. A couple of questions popped into my head while reading the Wings' words several hundred times and thought some of you might be asking similar questions.

The first questions that came to mind were what is the Lumes' world like and what about soul group levels higher than theirs? What happens to a soul that evolves beyond human life altogether? How far can we rise as souls? What happens when we reach the top?

This book discusses life and death as seen from one type of soul known as Wings. The Wings are the Seven Writers. The Unlit Souls didn't write it, which is one rung down the enlightenment ladder from Wings. Nor did the Lumes, which is one level up. Although the Wings briefly mention that there are levels higher than the Lumes, they don't discuss what happens on those planes of enlightenment at all. What I'm driving at here is that Seven Souls wrote a book about life in their world and their connection with their soul group members in this one. If we want to know about life beyond their world, your guess is as good as mine. This book is primarily about Wings. As far as my role is concerned, I'm simply the messenger. I'm little more than a "secretary to the souls", if you will, and just one of many people that write books on their behalf.

Having said that, I believe every word the souls wrote with all my heart. If not, I never would have put in the time and effort to type, organize and publish the many communications they shared over a period of several weeks more than eight years ago. Whether or not anyone else believes them boils down to faith or a lack of it, as far as I can see. You're either willing to believe what you've read here or you're not. Feel free to store your copy of the book in a time capsule to preserve it for posterity or light your next bonfire with it. The Seven Souls live in faith that the people who are meant to receive their message will do just that.

The other thing I'd like to address about the book is the amount of repetition within it. Why did the Wings repeat some information so often? The Wings used the words love and light and stressed the importance of learning how to

Lighten Up many times in their writings. Repeating the same information more than once or twice is normally considered taboo in a book. Repetition is how people learn, however, as you might recall from learning your multiplication tables in grade school. Although we've all heard that loving others is the secret to a happy life many times before, look how few of us have learned to apply those simple principles in our daily lives. Their message of living in faith and love is one that cannot be heard enough times.

This book is not intended to change the world overnight. It is designed to change the lives of some of the people that read it. How? By helping them understand that each and every life we touch is affected by our individual energy. Even one grain of sand is still a part of a huge beach. If even one person puts his or her best foot forward using faith and kindness every day, there will be a chain reaction. Why not choose to be that person? Show kindness to people and they will pass it along to others. The opposite also holds true. It's up to each of us to do our part, as small or insignificant as that might seem, in order to spread love in the world. We don't have to wait until we die to learn how to Lighten Up.

If enough people join the cause, the sky's the limit... literally.

This is where the ***Lighten Up*** book ends.

Continue here to read my unrepentant, shameless book plug. As mentioned earlier, I wrote a book called *3 Steps To Recovery*©, which was published in June, 2011. If you've heard the title before, congratulations! You are now a member of a society more secret than the Illuminati and more exclusive than Thurston Howell the Third's country club. The good news is that *3 Steps To Recovery*© has received more than twenty Five Star Amazon reader reviews and won a 2012 Reviewer's Choice Award.

3 Steps To Recovery© was written to help struggling addicts beat addiction through a spiritual awakening. I'm honored to report that it has accomplished that mission for long-term addicts and alcoholics around the globe. Because the *3 Steps*© have successfully helped people to change their lives, we decided to present them as an online teleclass, which we are preparing to launch soon.

If you'd like to experience a spiritual awakening/healing of your own, please visit www.3stepstorecovery.com or email Dan@3stepstorecovery.com.

You don't have to be an addict to attend classes, but if you are dealing with any type of addiction, anxiety, co-dependency, or other issues, then the *3 Steps To Spiritual Healing*™ course is for you.

If you are not struggling with trauma-related issues and simply wish to deepen your spiritual connection, the *3 Steps*

To Spiritual Awakening™ class is right up your alley. This course is like an adventure tour for the soul and for those that do experience a spiritual awakening, it is much like a taste of heaven.